BIRTH OF A SUCCESSFUL JOINT VENTURE

BIRTH OF A SUCCESSFUL JOINT VENTURE

The creation of
Nantong Cellulose Fibers Company
by
Jiangsu Tobacco Company,
of China National Tobacco Corporation
and
Celanese Fibers Operations,
a subsidiary of Hoechst/Celanese Corp.

Report written by
William H. Newman, Research Director
Center for Chinese Business Studies
Columbia University

Based on a joint study by
Graduate School of Business, Columbia University of
New York
and
Faculty of International Business Management,
University of International Business and Economics
(Beijing)

BIRTH OF A SUCCESSFUL JOINT VENTURE

• • •

William H. Newman

UNIVERSITY
PRESS OF
AMERICA

CENTER FOR
CHINESE
BUSINESS
STUDIES

Lanham • New York • London

Copyright © 1992 by
The Center for Chinese Business Studies

University Press of America®, Inc.
4720 Boston Way
Lanham, Maryland 20706

3 Henrietta Street
London WC2E 8LU England

Library of Congress Cataloging-in-Publication Data

Newman, William Herman, 1909–
Birth of a successful joint venture / by William H. Newman.
p.   cm.
Includes index.
1. Nantong Cellulose Fibers Company—History.
2. Cellulose industry—China.
3. Joint ventures—China—Case studies.
I. Title.
HD9660.C43C66   1992
338.7'677464'0951—dc20   92–10759 CIP

ISBN 0–8191–8723–2 (cloth : alk. paper)
ISBN 0–8191–8724–0 (pbk. : alk. paper)

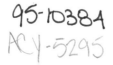

Acknowledgments

The study reported here is part of a broader effort by the Center for Chinese Business Studies of Columbia University in New York City, working in cooperation with the University of International Business and Economics in Beijing, to understand and assist in the development of business management in China.

Many people have contributed information and ideas bearing on this in-depth review of the launching of Nantong Cellulose Fibers Company. We especially want to thank the following persons for their help on this project.

From Celanese Fibers Operations (USA)

Edmond A. Collins	Michael Murphy
Michael Hazard	Donald H. Phillips
Vernon G. Kight	Richard H. Stofan
Lawrence J. Kilgore	Robert L. Stultz
Robert S. Molique	

From China National Tobacco Corporation and Jiangsu Tobacco Company

Jiang Ming	Xu Liyu
Jin Maoxian	Hu Gong Pu
Ma Erchi	Liu Kehei

From London Export Company

Katy Coe   Stephen Perry

From Nantong Cellulose Fibers Company

Roger Dysart   Wang Zhenhuan
James M. Stokes   Yao Guisheng
Wang Shouren   Zhu Xue-Quan

From University of International Business & Economics/Beijing

Gao Guopei   Xu Zijian
Ma Chunguang   Yu Qiang

From Columbia University in New York City

R. Randle Edwards   Hoke S. Simpson
Donald E. Sexton   N. T. Wang

The report which follows was written by Professor William H. Newman of Columbia University. My acquaintance with this impressive step in China's development comes from the diverse data generously contributed by the people listed above. However, responsibility for the selection of information and ideas to include in the report, for evaluations and inferences presented, and for the wording in English of ideas that may have unintended connotations in Chinese is mine. The report is a single person's view of a many-sided affair.

Contents

Executive Summary

1. The Nantong Cellulose Fibers Company, now in full operation, is headed for *outstanding success.* In spite of difficulties typically faced by joint ventures in developing countries, the new plant on the Yangtze River is already reducing the People's Republic of China's outlay of foreign exchange by millions of dollars.

Moreover, the founding partners—Hoechst Celanese Corporation and China National Tobacco Corporation—have already agreed to double the plant capacity and to build an acetate flake plant to produce the chief raw material.

2. Three initiatives were essential in building the successful Nantong joint venture: a) Both partners had to substantially modify their respective views of *the way the joint venture should be structured.* b) The *planning* that preceded the signing of the joint venture contract had to be much more *extensive and specific* than is usually done. c) The relationship between the partners had to move from suspicious bargaining to a *mutual concern* with finding practical ways *to cooperate* that would assure the economic soundness of the new venture.

Several years were required, but the result is a clear, focused venture that in many respects can serve as a model for other foreign joint ventures in developing countries.

3. The Nantong joint venture centers on the production of a single, conventional item—filter tow for cigarettes—in very large quantities.

China produces *1.5 trillion cigarettes each year*—about 30% of the world output, and is in the process of increasing the proportion of these cigarettes with filters from 10% to over 50%. Thousands of tons of filter material, called "tow," are needed.

Prior to the Nantong plant, all this tow was imported, involving a heavy drain on China's scarce foreign exchange. So, after an unsuccessful effort to obtain a simple technology transfer agreement, the P.R.C. opened its doors even wider by inviting proposals for joint ventures to produce tow locally.

4. In response, none of the international producers of tow was actively interested in a joint venture under the terms then offered by the Chinese. Although the general idea of a joint venture to produce tow seemed logical, when each side set terms based *only on its own interests* there was an *unsurmountable lack of fit.* Celanese, for example, initially decided to not even discuss a joint venture with the Chinese.

5. The deal had to be, not abandoned, but restructured. A sound joint venture was possible only when each prospective partner found *ways to serve the interests of the other partner* as well as its own. And to reach this modification in viewpoints, a respected mediator was necessary.

London Export Company played this crucial role. Often an agent for the P.R.C. and currently the agent for Celanese in the P.R.C., London Export was trusted by both prospective partners. A change in the way each side viewed the joint venture was achieved. For instance, the Chinese recognized import substitution as equivalent to new exports, and they agreed to immediately make Celanese a preferred supplier of tow; Celanese agreed to guarantee results of its technology, and to assist NCFC in keeping the technology up to date during the 15-year term of the joint venture contract.

With these and other changes aiding mutual benefit, the basic features of a joint venture agreement fell into place promptly. Under the revised arrangement, each party benefits and neither party is hurt by the success of the new venture—the Nantong Cellulose Fibers Company.

Without the help of London Export Company, it is doubtful that this joint venture would ever have been formed.

6. A strength of the Nantong Cellulose Fibers Company is its simplified role. During the early period when the Chinese were seeking tow

technology, the entire P.R.C. tobacco industry was being modernized under the China National Tobacco Corporation. Among many *improvements in efficiency* was the centralization of procurement of tow. This means, in effect, that the new joint venture does not have to market its output to over one hundred cigarette manufacturing plants. Also, domestic financing is simplified.

At the same time, Celanese provides R&D input for the joint venture.

Consequently, the Nantong plant can operate as a *"focused* factory," with a singular product line, an assured market, and state-of-the-art technology. The managers of the joint venture have time to learn modern management in a clear setting before they are dunked into a complex organization subject to frequent change.

7. Also, the present joint venture has *limited life* and is to be *self-liquidating.* After fifteen years Celanese receives termination compensation. The remaining business then belongs to a subsidiary of the China National Tobacco Corporation. Meanwhile, as a preferred supplier to its partner, Celanese expects to keep its U.S. tow plants running near capacity in spite of declining domestic demand. This gives Celanese a net cash inflow "up front."

For the joint venture company—the Nantong Cellulose Fibers Company—the significance of this limited life, self-liquidating feature is that the Nantong plant can remain an efficient, focused factory. Other joint undertakings, which are not unlikely in view of the success of the present venture, can be set up as separate ventures each with its own appropriate design. Thus, adaptability to new opportunities can come through a series of separate ventures tailored to specific needs, instead of trying to have one company serve diverse situations.

8. To assure a workable agreement between the partners, the joint venture contract was much more comprehensive and specific than is typical. *Troublesome questions were confronted and resolved* rather than postponed "to be considered later" as is common in China. Plans for the new plant were carried through to layouts and equipment specifications, with lists of who would supply each item.

Significantly, to achieve this *refined planning* the tone of the discussions shifted from bargaining to "how can we cooperate most effectively." At this stage, the focus was on improving results, since the basis for dividing the benefits had already been set.

9. Innovative contract provisions that might cause delay in securing approval of government agencies were discussed with key people in

the controlling agencies prior to submission of a finished document. To this extent, *approval moved concurrently with the writing of the joint venture contract.* The aim was to achieve national goals but not necessarily through the means presented in standard regulations.

The impact of the reviewing agencies was not reduced in this approach. Instead, their influence took place earlier than usual while the whole design was taking shape. Thus, uncertainty was reduced and the time required for approval of formal documents was shortened.

10. Good *"boundary spanners"* are very important in designing and launching a foreign joint venture. A boundary spanner serves as a bridge between both sides of an issue. He/she *understands, empathizes with, is trusted, and can communicate* with key individuals whose interests in a proposed action differ sharply. More specifically for the Nantong Cellulose Fibers joint venture, boundary spanners were crucial in restructuring the basic elements in the foreign/China agreement; they were necessary in working through the specific provisions of the joint venture contract; they played important roles in reaching agreement between government and company officials; and boundary spanning was needed, but turned out to be inadequate, in linking service organizations and the new company during the construction phase.

Boundary spanning which involves two countries such as China and the United States calls for unusual skill. It is likewise important in China where tradition calls for great deference between levels in formal organizations.

11. Most troublesome in the launching of Nantong Cellulose Fibers Company was the interaction between founders of the company and several service groups such as design institutes and building contractors. North Americans assumed that when a company hires a service organization to perform a specified task the service organization had a professional obligation to help the company to the best of its ability. At least two of the *primary service groups* employed for the Nantong venture did not appear to have a high level of customer orientation. They were mostly concerned with their own convenience and maintaining good relations with central authorities in Beijing.

Incentives that will encourage these service groups to join in a team effort need to be devised.

12. The future of the Nantong Cellulose Fibers Company depends only partly on economic factors. As already noted, the domestic de-

mand for tow is so large that demand for the Nantong plant's output promises to be unusually stable throughout the fifteen-year period of the joint venture contract. Not so clear is *how the plant will be maintained.* It can become a showplace of China's modernization, maintained with a cleanliness befitting a computer chip laboratory. It should not be permitted to run down, thereby making the steady output of quality products hard to sustain. Running a "tight ship" must become traditional in China—as it is in, say, Switzerland.

13. Looking at the Nantong Cellulose Fibers Company more broadly, the design of this enterprise suggests a pattern for *"progressive venturing."* The present company has a limited life, but it can become a prototype for an array of comparable joint ventures. Each separate venture would have a clear, simple mission—and be structured so that it was economically self-sufficient during its limited life. Overhead would be low and the venture would focus on doing its particular task outstandingly well.

Flexibility and growth would come from a *succession* of such joint ventures, each tailor-made to fit new opportunities. As old ventures were liquidated new ones would be created. Thus, the total system would evolve, but the individual units would be highly efficient during their limited, focused lives.

14. Indeed, such a pattern of progressive venturing is already underway in the Celanese Fibers Operation-China National Tobacco Corporation relationship. Agreements have been reached to a) double the capacity of the Nantong tow plant, and b) build a twenty-five thousand ton acetate flake plant that will provide the chief raw material for the expanded tow operations. The mutual trust and the working out of acceptable bases for cooperative action—that emerged from the first venture—created a setting in which the next steps could be taken with confidence.

Introduction

Chapter 1

Learning From A Sound Venture

Joint ventures are often attractive, sometimes rewarding, and always difficult.

Each of these characteristics is magnified in a Chinese/foreign equity joint venture—such as the one analyzed in depth in the following pages.

The Appeal of Joint Ventures

Foreign joint ventures are a device for bringing together three world-shaping trends:

a. Modernization of China. The People's Republic of China is in the process of bringing almost a fourth of the world's population to a fourfold increase in standard of living. The magnitude and speed of this change is unmatched in human history. Spurred on by Japan, South Korea, Taiwan, and Hong Kong—mainland China is seeking modern technology from Western countries.

b. Globalization of international trade. The concept of trade between separate nations is changing sharply. Speeded-up communications, travel and transportation have made possible a closer integration of the flow of goods and services. Multiple sources and multiple markets now call for all sorts of dynamic realignments. Large corporations can no longer flourish in isolated territories; instead, they must position themselves to deal with world supply and demand. And in this enlarged arena China is emerging as a significant potential player.

c. New forms of cooperative effort. The scramble for new competitive positions, coupled with rapid technological and social change, has fostered a wide array of cooperative efforts. Joint sharing of skills and resources often permits a faster response than each company acting alone. And "joint ventures" are one form of this accelerating cooperation.

When combined, these three trends are synergistic. China's push for modernization opens the door for global companies seeking a position, however modest, in that huge potential market. The global companies can provide the technology and access to foreign demand which China urgently needs. And joint ventures serve as a mechanism for integrating these three potent trends.

Nantong Cellulose Fibers Company, the subject of our study, illustrates the way these three trends reinforce each other. For the 1.5 trillion cigarettes smoked each year, China wants to increase the numbers with filters; this will help to (1) meet the high domestic demand, (2) serve health and fiscal purposes, and (3) modernize its cigarette production. U.S. Celanese Fibers Operations with its mature domestic market and resulting rising interest in world markets can provide technology and training to help China fulfill locally its needs for cigarette filters. And a joint venture is the mechanism for joining China's need with Celanese's capability. A model of the way these forces fit together is shown in Exhibit 1-1.

Moving from Broad Concepts to a Sound Operating Company

Broad concepts, however appealing, are not enough. As illustrated in this study of the Nantong Cellulose Fibers Company, a whole series of steps are critical in moving from an idea for a joint venture to an actual operating company with quality products flowing from its ship-

EXHIBIT 1-1
Joint Venture Model

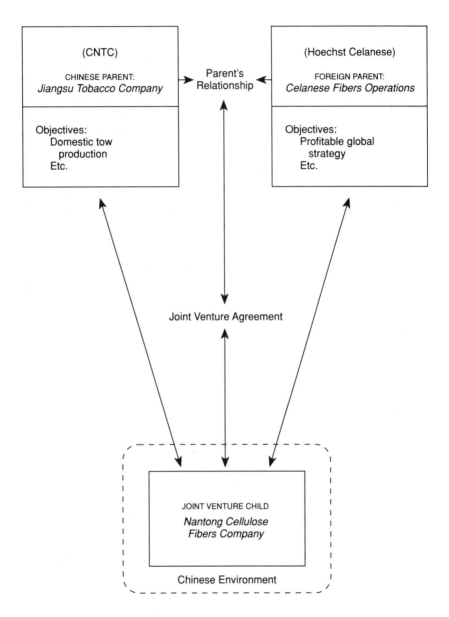

Adapted from K. R. Harrigan, *Strategies for Joint Ventures* (Lexington, MA: Lexington Books, 1985).

ping platform. Indeed, most potential joint ventures fail during the transition process. When two distinct cultures must be meshed together in a joint venture, as is inevitable in a Chinese/foreign equity joint venture, the transition is especially hazardous.

Government regulations that are not in tune with economic realities may block negotiations. The long-run objectives of the founding partners often clash, and resolutions of these differences must be found. Chinese and Western approaches to employee relations differ. Multilingual personnel who can bridge two diverse cultures are scarce, especially when they must also understand the technology and industry structure in which the joint venture will operate. Perceptions of risks and rewards may spring from very different bases. Yet a sound joint venture must find ways to deal with these and similar obstacles.

In addition, the close cooperation inherent in a joint venture calls for at least acceptable resolution of a host of quite specific operating problems. An intriguing joint venture concept can break down over relatively detailed questions such as these:

1. When is the piping in a new chemical plant to be tested for small leaks—before or after the insulation is put on? (A construction contract was jeopardized on this seemingly simple issue.)

2. Who decides on the allocation of operating income between a larger contribution to the workers' welfare fund and more dividends (in scarce foreign exchange) paid to the U.S. parent?

3. How can foreign managers (whose families are expected to live in provincial cities like Nantong) be motivated while working alongside Chinese employees whose living standards are equitable in the Chinese system but perceived by foreigners as being below U.S. standards?

Clearly, the *range* of issues involved in launching a successful Chinese joint venture is very wide.

Distinctiveness of Present Study

This report differs from most other discussions of Chinese/foreign joint ventures in several ways:

- It focuses on a successful joint venture. The American press tends to feature bad news rather than good news. At least with respect to Chinese joint ventures, reports of breakdowns have predominated. The Nantong Cellulose Fibers Company, in contrast, has found ways to overcome the main obstacles that it faced.

- A broad range of issues is covered. The report deals with the background and development of the concept of the company, the tedious process of negotiating the joint venture agreement, and a representative sample of problems in constructing the plant and getting it into operation. And the impact of the early stages in the process on the later ones are noted.

- Several points of view are considered. We have talked with key people in each of the sponsoring organizations, and with the managers who are putting the joint venture agreement into effect. The report is not a one-sided story.

Purpose and Method of Study

An aim of this study is to help other prospective and existing joint venture participants to see, in depth, the process of launching a successful joint venture. As already noted, this process can contribute substantially to the economic development of China. Also, it can aid foreign partners in their repositioning to play an active role in the evolving global competition.

A related aim is to look more specifically at the complexity and hurdles involved in getting a Chinese joint venture into effective operation. Although we have focused on a single example, several possible guidelines (do's and don't's) for dealing with typical problems do emerge.

The joint venture that we studied to achieve these aims was launched by the China National Tobacco Corporation and Celanese Corporation, headquartered in the United States. Celanese is one of the world suppliers of "tow," the inside material of cigarette filters. China National Tobacco Corporation (CNTC) invited Celanese to participate in the construction and operation of a large tow plant in Nantong, China—a provincial city on the north side of the Yangtze River about ninety miles from Shanghai.

The direct parents of the emerging joint venture, however, are operating divisions of the two larger corporations—Jiangsu Tobacco Company for CNTC, and Celanese Fibers Operations, Ltd. for Celanese Corporation. The full name of the joint venture is Nantong Cellulose Fibers Company, Limited (NCFC).

(During the time covered by the study, Celanese Corporation was acquired by Hoechst A.G. of Frankfurt, Germany, and the name was changed to Hoechst/Celanese. However, Hoechst A.G. was not active in the cigarette tow business, and the merger had no direct impact on the development of the joint venture. So, in this report we follow industry practice of referring to the foreign parent simply as "Celanese.")

The period covered by our study extends from the early 1980s, when the Chinese first became actively interested in acquiring tow manufacturing capability from foreign sources, up to the fall of 1989 when the Nantong tow plant finally started full-scale operations.

Our study of NCFC was a tiny joint venture in itself. Representatives of the Graduate School of Business, Columbia University (New York) did the interviewing of English-speaking managers and experts involved in developing the joint venture. Representatives of the Faculty of International Business Management, University of International Business and Economics (Beijing) did the interviewing of Chinese-speaking managers and government officials. Both groups examined relevant published material in English and Chinese. An encouraging note relative to the validity of the data is that while various individuals commented on different parts of the total story, no significant inconsistencies about what happened emerged from our numerous sources.

(A full list of the persons interviewed appears in the "Acknowledgments" in the front of the report. However, within the report we will avoid indicating who said what.)

Organization of the Report

Three stages stand out in the development of the NCFC joint venture. First, from 1982 to the middle of 1984 the conception of the basic features of the cooperation evolved. Both CNTC and Celanese changed their thinking during this period. Although in hindsight two-plus years seems like a long time before the two parents were willing to even start negotiations, the learning that occurred during this stage was a crucial contributor to a workable agreement. As explained in Part I of the report, launching the joint venture waited—wisely we believe—until consideration switched from just a technology transfer to a joint venture and both parents were more realistic in their basic expectations and demands.

The second stage, described in Part II, was the prolonged negotiation of the joint venture agreement. A distinctive feature of this process was the effort to express clearly what each partner would contribute to the joint undertaking. Most troublesome issues were confronted, not hidden in vague language. Plans were developed in greater detail than occurs in many other joint venture contracts. Concurrence was secured at both the local level and the national level. Such agreements often were not easy to reach, as will be noted in Chapters 7 through 11. But the resulting joint venture contract has a high probability of being executed without frequent and even bitter renegotiations.

Construction and start-up of the plant, the third stage that is reviewed in Part III, put inter-cultural cooperation to the test. Even the well developed plans highlighted in Parts I and II ran into occasional snags. Most of these difficulties arose because of unexpected or unacceptable differences in cultural practices. Again, significant learning how to work together has taken place, but the short-run associations of construction crews and construction supervisors leaves doubt about how much of this learning can be transferred to the regular work force and managers.

At the close of chapters or Parts, a tentative set of guidelines for future joint venture negotiations and managers are presented. Although we hesitate to generalize from one example, the NCFC case is distinctive enough to warrant close attention. We hope that readers will agree that a provocative attempt to generalize is better than drawing no inferences at all.

Part I

Slow Birth of a Practical Concept

A "good deal"—clearly beneficial to each of the founding partners—is the heart of a sound joint venture. The venture itself is inherently fragile; each partner is pursuing its own agenda, and these agendas will change over time. The new organization needs continuing strength to survive in its own bailiwick. So, unless the venture creates strong benefits it may never be born, let alone survive.

Our analysis of joint ventures in China indicates that this elementary requirement is frequently missing. Too often a venture is launched merely on the identification of an attractive project, without thinking through inputs and outputs for each partner.

The Celanese/China National Tobacco Corporation joint venture is a good example of the difficulty in finding a way to structure the cooperative effort so that each partner clearly gains. CNTC's original concept, which was based on unclear expectations in China's central government about technology transfers, was rejected by all possible foreign partners. And for several years Celanese would consider only sale of products, not technology, to yet another potential competitor in the world market. A reshaped concept of the basis for working together was needed, as well as revised perspectives by each partner. This first step took over two years—and skillful mediation between the partners by a trusted advisor to both partners.

Until this core concept was developed and accepted, trying to negotiate the more specific features of a joint venture would have been only sparring and futile. In the case described in this report, and we suspect for most other equity joint ventures, thinking through the central unifying structure must come first.

The way such a unifying concept was developed for what is now Nantong Cellulose Fibers Company, Limited, is described in the following chapters.

Chapter 2   Tow—A Step in China's Modernization
Chapter 3   Seeking Help from a Global Industry
Chapter 4   Celanese: Reluctant Prospective Partner
Chapter 5   Developing a Sound Basis for Joint Action
Chapter 6   Conclusion of Part I—Developing a Workable Conception of the Joint Venture

Chapter 2

Tow—A Step In China's Modernization

A business joint venture, like any other company, can survive only when it creates a product or service which is in strong demand. In the case of Nantong Cellulose Fibers Company (NCFC) the product is clearly defined. NCFC makes and sells only a single type of product— "tow"—in vast quantities. As explained in the previous chapter, tow is the major component in cigarette filters. And making cellulose acetate tow is what NCFC is all about.

China's demand for tow is not so simply defined.

China Decision to Manufacture Filter Cigarettes

By the mid-1970s Chinese people—mostly men—were smoking hundreds of billions of cigarettes each year. Smoking had become a primary way in the Chinese environment to relax a bit, to take a break; also offering a cigarette to another person was a widespread friendly gesture; it was one of the amenities of life that most people could afford.

The demand for tow, however, was delayed until 1978 when—in keeping with its broad modernization program—the government first decided to put filters on a small number of locally made cigarettes. This experiment triggered a major thrust to increase the percentage of Chinese cigarettes that have filters. Suddenly the *potential* market for tow jumped dramatically. Millions of dollars (or equivalent in other currency) might be involved.

Three important reasons supported the decision to put filters on more of China's cigarettes.

1. Filter cigarettes symbolize the thrust to modernize the Chinese cigarette industry. No longer will "world-class" filter cigarettes be available only in very costly imports. China's own products will be among the best. And the widespread use of cigarettes in China means that this symbol of modernization will be conspicuous throughout the nation.

2. Adding filters fits with the government's continuing concern about personal health. Some studies suggest that smoking cigarettes with filters reduces the long-run risk of respiratory and other diseases.

3. Since filter cigarettes sell for higher prices than regular brands, the government's stream of tax receipts will be enhanced somewhat by the up-grading. And the central government's income from tax on tobacco products is a significant item in the total budget.

4. The addition of a filter reduces the quantity of tobacco in a cigarette. So, adding filters cuts the total amount of tobacco leaf needed. This reduction, in turn, frees up agricultural land for other crops such as food.

This unusual combination of supporting factors makes an increase in the proportion of cigarettes that have filters particularly desirable to the central government. In fact, the share of filter cigarettes has increased to over 40% by the late 1980s, and government officials have referred to a 50%—or even 90%—target. (Note that 50% of the more than 1.5 trillion cigarettes produced in China in 1988 is a larger market than exists in the entire United States where the ratio of cigarettes with filters is over 95%. See Exhibit 2-1 on world production of cigarettes.)

In passing, we might note here that Celanese had been a participant in China's increasing use of filters since the beginning. Through the initiative of London Export Company (Celanese's agent in China), Celanese made the first significant shipment of tow into China in 1980/81, and also provided filter rod-making machines and engineering advice for making filter cigarettes. That gesture was almost a decade prior to the opening of China's first domestic tow plant.

The Decision to Build Domestic Tow Plants

The sharp increase in filter cigarettes comes with a cost. Currently, all the tow must be imported. Over 125,000 tons of tow will be needed when the government's target of 50% filter cigarettes is met. Assuming a landed cost (purchase price plus shipping, insurance, import tax, etc.) of $4,000 per ton, the total outlay would become about $600 million per year.

Most of that substantial sum would have to be paid in foreign exchange—hard currency—if China continues to rely on imports. And this is an outlay that China can ill afford. China's limited supply of foreign exchange is urgently needed for machinery and technical assistance in building a new internal communication system, improving internal transportation, expanding electrical power, modernizing health facilities, and a variety of other infra-structure and productivity needs. Allocations of foreign exchange for tow face severe competition with other modernization needs.

The obvious resolution of this foreign exchange constraint on expanding the use of tow is to make tow within China. The benefits listed on page 14 are economically and politically feasible only if most of the necessary supply of tow comes from domestic plants. So, by 1982–83 when filter cigarettes were still less than 10% of China's total output, provision for construction of two plants was included in the national plan. Indeed, the central planning continued to the stage of selecting locations for such prospective plants (Nantong, Jilin or Xian).

Recognition in the complex plan for a huge country like China is a long, long way from having plants which are actually producing the identified product. Nevertheless, such recognition made the formation of NCFC possible within the 1980s. If a plan to produce tow in China had to be added to an existing national plan, instead of already being a

EXHIBIT 2-1
World Production of Cigarettes, 1988

Leading countries		Production in billions*
China		1,544
United States		693
USSR		391
Japan		265
West Germany		169
	Total for top five	3,062
All other countries		2,255
	World total	5,317

* Includes cigarettes produced for export.

part of that plan, long delay for assessment would have been faced. Being part of China's prevailing modernization plan is a great aid to any joint venture—as our review in Part II of NCFC's creation will show.

Formation of China National Tobacco Corporation (CNTC)

Every business enterprise is dependent on reliable external linkages. A distribution network to reach consumers is essential. Also vital are ties to suppliers of resources—materials, labor, capital, government licenses and support, etc. An enterprise cannot survive alone. It must have dependable links with its economic and political environment.

A joint venture like NCFC is no exception to this basic need for predictable and reliable relationships with consumers and resource suppliers. However, as a joint venture NCFC can get some help from the corporations that formed it. And NCFC is especially fortunate in the ability of its Chinese "parent" to provide such help.

If NCFC had been established in, say, 1980 it would have had to sell its output of tow to some or all of the over one hundred separate cigarette factories then in operation. And it would have been in a weak position to get foreign exchange and favorable tax consideration. Fortunately for NCFC, a tobacco monopoly and its administrative arm, China National Tobacco Corporation, were created in 1982 and were in full operation by July 1984 when Celanese decided to consider a joint venture to make tow in China. Without CNTC's consolidation of the entire tow market, Celanese would have stayed out of China.

CNTC is the instrument for modernizing the whole tobacco industry in China. Filter cigarettes, and plants to make the tow for filters, are only one dimension of a concerted move to modernize an entire widespread industry. Because CNTC is so important to the economic feasibility of any joint venture to make tow in China, we should briefly describe these benefits.

Starting about 1982 the State Council (top executive organ of the People's Republic of China) has shaped the tobacco industry as a national monopoly. The State Council declared that all branches of the industry will be unified as a centrally governed monopoly, and that China National Tobacco Corporation will be the administrative arm—reporting directly to the State Council—to manage this almost unique form of organization. The activities in the monopoly cover:

> . . . all activities related to the production and sale of tobacco, cigarettes, cigars, and smoking tobacco—including plantation, purchase, and processing of leaf tobacco; production and sale of cigarettes; pricing; trademark registration; transportation; production and distribution of cigarette paper, filters, and cigarette manufacturing equipment; international trade; and economic and technical cooperation with foreign countries.

Basically, all of the foregoing activities that formerly were in ministries and administrations have been transferred to CNTC; this includes tobacco bureaus, institutes, and plants formerly under the supervision of government of the provinces and separate municipalities.

The activities assigned to CNTC are so broad in scope and cover such a large geographic area, planning and controls in some activities are still being refined. The control of leaf production and of tax receipts, for instance, have been troublesome in some localities. Nevertheless, CNTC has made major advances in reducing the number of small inefficient plants, improving the quality of cigarettes sold, and increasing tax receipts. The modernization of the industry is moving ahead impressively.

This recent development of CNTC has helped in the creation of Celanese's joint venture with Jiangsu Tobacco Company (a provincial tobacco company under the supervision of CNTC) in two crucial ways.

1. CNTC can provide NCFC with an assured market for its output of tow. Without CNTC's production scheduling and allocation of a scarce material like tow, NCFC would have to establish a marketing department to deal with perhaps 100 plants of diverse size and sophistication. Now, in effect NCFC turns over its marketing problems to CNTC.

2. With CNTC's backing, NCFC's bargaining position with other government bodies is both simplified and strengthened. The number of endorsements necessary to get the joint venture launched has been sharply reduced. For instance, London Export Company (Celanese's agent in China) listed over twenty ministries and administrative bodies whose concurrence would have been necessary just prior to CNTC's birth. In contrast, by 1986 that number had been cut in half. (See Exhibit 2-2.) Moreover, the creation of CNTC and its position reporting directly to the State Council shows in advance a strong backing by the State Council. This evidence of support assists in obtaining approval of plans for production and financing.

The task of forming a coalition supporting a joint venture to produce tow—without CNTC in the picture—would have been extremely difficult to put together. For instance, the Ministry of Light Industry might have sponsored the plant at Nantong but would be in a weak position to help coordinate marketing and the supply of tobacco. Or, the Chemical Ministry might have devised a plan to produce tow in a large chemical complex (e.g., at Jilin) but would be even more remote from tobacco supply and cigarette marketing than the Ministry of Light Industry. Celanese—or any other foreign company—would have faced much higher risk and the negotiating period would have been much longer with any of the other partners. With CNTC in existence, a strong structure for coordinated action had already been established.

Linking the Tow Program with National Policy

Modernizing the tobacco industry, including domestic production of tow for filter cigarettes, is only one of an array of efforts to bring China's standard of living up to "developed" country levels. And on almost all fronts Western technology is a much needed input. Especially after the end of the "cultural revolution" and opening the

EXHIBIT 2-2
Important Chinese Government Agencies
Directly Involved with the Cigarette Industry

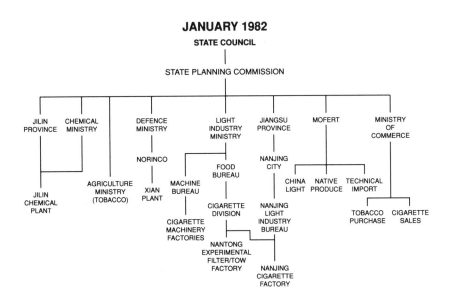

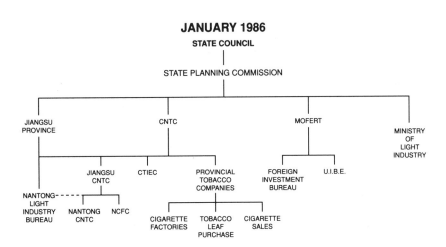

Source: China Business Services, Ltd.

boundaries to ideas from the West, modern technology has been viewed as almost a magic wand for raising productivity.

The central government has been experimenting with ways of obtaining modern technology. Technology for making tow is at the forefront of these efforts. An early approach has been simply to buy technology from a Western company. This has had very limited success because a) technology involves much more than a set of blueprints or machines, b) few companies are willing to part with their know-how on the terms offered by the Chinese, and c) China lacks the foreign exchange to pay for more than a fraction of its technology needs.

To overcome this last hurdle, a formidable condition has been attached to most technology transfers—foreign exchange to pay for the purchase must be obtained from sales of the resulting China-produced products on the world market. Then, since few Chinese companies can suddenly become world-class suppliers, joint ventures have to be authorized as a form of organization that may attract foreign suppliers of modern technology.

In the next chapter we shall review how the world suppliers of tow responded to these proposed structures for transferring technology. The point to note here is that acquiring technology is a broad problem for China. The government policy guiding such transfers is both new and evolving. Laws and regulations to implement the new policies are just emerging. But some generalized regulations do exist, and conscientious bureaucrats do try to apply them to specific proposals for technology transfers.

Consequently, the transfer of tow production technology is not treated as a unique problem. Even a monopoly organization such as CNTC must fit its technology acquisitions into an emerging set of regulations.

Being part of a major modernization movement has helped in the formation of the NCFC joint venture, especially in the strengths that CNTC provides. At the same time being part of a pioneering effort is a slow process because the rules of the game are still crude and unsettled, and government officials are still learning how to apply them.

*   *   *

For cigarette filters, then, the Chinese market is very large and very strong. Moreover, this market is centralized under CNTC's guidance. So, "marketing" in the Western sense is simple—the main hurdle being foreign exchange. The supply side of the picture, in contrast, poses major hurdles—which the following chapters will describe.

Chapter 3

Seeking Help From a Global Industry

Joint ventures call for action—action by the two companies forming the venture, and action by the venture itself. A decision by one corporation such as CNTC to seek a joint venture is only a start. The circumstances in China prompting CNTC to make that start were sketched in the preceding chapter. The present chapter explains difficulties CNTC had in finding a partner also eager to take action.

Another look at the joint-venture model, Figure 1-1, highlights how discriminating each partner in a joint venture needs to be. A mutual interest is necessary but insufficient. The specific goals of each partner, the contributions he is able and willing to make, other perhaps competing commitments, inducements (benefits) that will have to be provided, relative power of the partners, trust and dependability and other values guiding each partner's actions, flexibility and willingness to adapt to changing conditions—all must be weighed.

And as one partner looks skeptically at the other, each will be forced to look inward as well. Often one's own stance has to be adjusted if compatibility is to be achieved.

In the Nantong Cellulose Fibers Company example, the Chinese took the initiative in seeking a joint-venture partner. So, we will first review their efforts, and then look at the responses they received. In spite of the potential benefits to both partners, this example was not a case of love at first sight!

Who Was Actually the Chinese Suitor

The designation of Jiangsu Tobacco Company as the Chinese partner in a joint venture to produce tow evolved through several stages. That role was not clear-cut when contacts with foreign companies were first started. In 1981 when the decision to produce tow in China was endorsed by the central planner, only a technology purchase contract was contemplated.

Three potential sites for tow plants were eventually selected: Nantong which had good water transportation and was designated for industrial development; Jilin where tow production could be incorporated into a large existing chemical complex; and Xian where NORINCO, a business entity of the People's Liberation Army, was to be a partner in the tow joint venture. There was tentative agreement to start at Nantong (in Jiangsu Province) because of better access to world shipping, and some experimental research on the production of tow had been done there.

A team was formed to make a world tour a) to learn more about the foreign tow producers and their technology, and b) to look for a company that would sell to the Chinese the most modern technology for producing tow. However, at this time CNTC had not yet been formed, so the team consisted of people from several different organizations. The team included representatives from the Cigarette Division of the Ministry of Light Industry, the Tobacco Import and Export section of the Ministry of Foreign Economic Relations and Trade, the Jiangsu Tobacco Company, the Shanghai Light Industry Engineering Design Institute, and others.

While this team did learn a lot about the world tow industry, a vital conclusion reached in 1982 was that no major producer of tow was interested in selling technology to China. Several reasons probably led each of the foreign producers to the same decision:

1. The terms of the standardized technology transfer contract which the Chinese were trying to use at that time were quite unrealistic from

the foreigner's viewpoint—at least for tow technology. A modest cash payment was clearly inadequate.

2. The Chinese were vague about how extensively the technology would be used inside and outside of China, and about the availability of the support structure necessary to make sophisticated equipment run up to the output levels which the foreign supplier was expected to guarantee.

3. By 1982 worldwide tow production capacity was starting to exceed demand, and the existing firms did not want to contribute to additional capacity that was likely to upset the balance between supply and demand even more.

In other words, at this stage the central government in China was making real progress in internal plans for the tobacco industry but knowledge about the attitudes and expectations of foreign tow producers was weak. Also, the Chinese internal organization lacked an operating unit that had the authority and resources to work effectively with a specific foreign company on the business and technical operation of a plant. In American slang, "The Chinese did not have their act together."

A Shift from Only Technology Transfer to Joint Venture

By 1983 the Chinese were ready to try a revised approach to foreign tow producers. Differences in the Chinese position included:

1. A joint venture with a foreign partner was now possible. Because of frequent difficulties with inducing different sorts of foreign companies to sell technology for a fee, the central government issued new regulations allowing joint ventures. This made it possible for the foreign company to share in the longer-term benefits from using a transferred technology in China. Moreover, the foreign company established at least indirectly a presence in China that might be helpful in other transactions.

2. CNTC was established and could provide coordinated marketing and allocating of the output of a local tow plant throughout China. Also, CNTC was in a stronger position than previous enterprises to

obtain foreign exchange to cover enterprises to obtain foreign exchange to cover repatriation of fees, offshore expenses, and profits if and when earned.

3. A specific plant site in Nantong had been selected with the cooperation of the local government. Nantong is on the Yangtze River, allowing direct shipments by barge of coal, acetate flake, and other materials.

4. And by 1984 CNTC was prepared to use the foreign partner in a joint venture as a preferred supplier of tow or acetate flake until plants producing local supplies were on-stream—provided the foreign partner met international standards for quality and price.

These revisions of the contract provisions that the Chinese—now clearly CNTC—were prepared to offer a foreign joint venture partner represented a major advance toward a workable cooperative deal. Both CNTC and the central planning organizations were shifting from looking only at domestic needs and attitudes to also adjusting to foreign company needs.

A team of Chinese officials set out in August 1983 on a world tour to learn the level of cellulose acetate tow production at the major producers, to understand more about the technology and equipment used in such production, and to determine under what conditions would the major producers cooperate in China. Organized by the China Technology Import and Export Corporation, this twelve-member team included representatives of NORINCO, CNTC, Jiangsu Tobacco Company, Shanghai Light Industry Design Institute, and others.

Although the consolidation of the tobacco industry under CNTC was still going on when the second team made its tour, membership of the team reflected the strong monopoly movement. Moreover, securing close control over an expanding availability of tow within China would further strengthen CNTC's control of high-quality cigarettes throughout China. Domestic tow production had become an integral feature of the national plan for the tobacco industry. So, the search for a foreign partner had significance beyond a convenient way to save foreign exchange.

World Suppliers of Tow

Realistically, a foreign partner in a Chinese joint venture has to be one of the existing world suppliers of tow. These are the companies that have the specific production know-how which the Chinese need.

Tow is made by a chemical process similar to the production of rayon or other synthetic yarns. It is a large-scale, capital intensive process that must run continuously twenty-four hours a day. The main raw material is cellulose acetate flake, which typically comes from wood pulp. (Alternative chemical bases have not proven to be practical.)

All major suppliers of tow use substantially the same process. Changes in the size and number of strands going into a filter rod can be made relatively easily. As a result, tow made by one producer can be substituted for that of other producers, and tow is sold worldwide as a commodity. The combination of substitutability and high fixed costs associated with the capital intensive process leads to sharp competition in the international market.

While several countries have small plants that produce tow for internal consumption, most of the tow in international trade comes from six companies located in four countries:

Celanese	
Tennessee Eastman	United States
Daicel	
Mitsubishi	Japan
Deutsche Rhodia	Germany
Courtaulds	Great Britain

Joint venture partners for CNTC to produce tow in China will probably come from this group of six companies. The Chinese study team investigated all of them on its second world-tour.

Foreign Interest in a Joint Venture in China

The joint venture concept, in contrast to just a technology transfer sale, stirred positive responses from half of CNTC's potential partners.

The most active interest came from Eastman, which had just signed a color film technology contract with Xiamen Photographic Materials Company and China National Technology Import and Export Corporation. Under the guidance of Eastman's Hong Kong office and assisted by the Shanghai Light Industry Institute for Design Engineering, a team of Americans was sent to Beijing to explore the possibilities. This response was encouraging to CNTC, but the discussions remained at the exploratory level. The American representatives were technical people who hesitated to state Eastman's position clearly; the Shanghai Institute and Hong Kong representatives, on the other hand, assumed that they could design a plant that needed only an okay from Eastman's headquarters in the United States.

Daicel expressed strong interest in cooperation. Their priority in discussions, however, centered on sales of tow while production capacity in China was being developed. Also, a reluctance to make substantial fixed investments in China was evident. Perhaps because the investment in Xian might be lower, Daicel showed interest in that location rather than Nantong.

Deutsche Rhodia responded favorably to the idea of a joint venture, but was unable to follow up promptly at that time (early 1984).

The other three potential partners—Mitsubishi, Courtaulds, and Celanese—stuck to the negative position they had taken on the earlier technology transfer inquiry. At least for Celanese, CNTC explicitly asked for a proposal. Within Celanese, opinion was divided on how to respond. Nevertheless, senior management held to the view that Celanese should not help to expand world tow production capacity, especially when a surplus currently existed; instead, Celanese would be better off concentrating on selling the output of its present plants. Consequently, in March 1984 Celanese notified CNTC that it was not interested in discussing a joint venture.

Lessons for an Impatient Deal Maker

Clearly, notable progress had been made in CNTC's search for foreign help in establishing domestic production of tow. In the three years from 1981 to early 1984 foreign companies had moved from no interest to three large firms at least considering a joint venture. However, in terms of the conditions necessary for a sound joint venture, briefly listed at the beginning of this chapter, large gaps in a mutual agreement remained.

Even the most advanced negotiations with a potential joint venture partner were too narrow in scope. Discussions had focused mostly on the technology to be transferred and the design of a plant. Capital contributions by each partner and the top managerial structure, both critical components in a joint venture agreement, remained vague generalities. More serious, a close working relationship—mutual trust—between senior managers in the potential foreign partner and the CNTC appeared to be slow in developing. Also relationships with officials in Nantong had not been developed. So, a basis for cooperatively working together had not yet been created.

Looking back on the three-year period 1981 to 1984, it is clear that social learning takes time. A Chinese goal, domestic production of tow, was accepted in 1981, but realistic ideas on how to achieve that goal were slow in emerging. Both a) practical concepts on how to build cooperation with foreign companies, and b) a favorable internal organization structure had to evolve. Delay was costly in terms of foreign exchange. However, the establishment of CNTC was a substantial change in government structure, and acceptance of foreigners as active participants in internal economic activity reversed a basic attitude that had been a tenet in the communist revolution doctrine. It is impressive that modifications of this sort could occur in only three years.

Nevertheless, without these modifications substantial foreign help with local production of tow would have been impossible.

A related change on the part of potential foreign partners was also necessary. Here the unresolved issues were long-term versus short-term return on technological know-how and managerial effort, a potential restructuring of competition, and an assessment of the risks of doing business in the People's Republic of China.

Chapter 4

Celanese: Reluctant Prospective Partner

Celanese, the foreign company that eventually did join CNTC in building the first acetate cigarette tow plant in China, was slow in responding to CNTC's invitation to discuss a joint venture. In fact, Celanese almost passed up the opportunity.

The reasons for this delay by the two parents of Nantong Cellulose Fibers Company in entering discussions, and then their moving energetically to negotiate a carefully conceived agreement, illustrate the depth of commitment needed in a successful joint venture. The relationship should not be undertaken casually.

Attractiveness of Celanese as a Partner

From the start of its search for a partner, CNTC regarded Celanese as a good prospect. At a minimum CNTC hoped Celanese would submit one of the three competing proposals that the State Council requires before a major contract is approved. The attractions of Celanese included the following points:

1. Celanese is a strong, major competitor in the international market for tow. Its production costs are at least comparable to other major suppliers; this implies that the technology know-how that Celanese would provide would be as good as any available. Also, Celanese has the financial and manpower strength to undertake another large project such as producing tow, and perhaps acetate flake, in China. No competitor of Celanese has greater strength in the tow industry. (The merger of Celanese with Hoechst A. G. of Frankfurt, Germany, in 1986 added to the financial strength backing Celanese Fibers Operations, Inc. Otherwise, Celanese tow activities were not directly affected by the merger because Hoechst had not been in the tow business.)

2. Celanese had been a regular supplier of cellulose acetate cigarette filter tow to China since the early 1980s. In fact, Celanese sent the first shipment of such tow to China, along with two machines for making filter rods and some technical advisors to teach the Chinese how to run the machines!
Also, Celanese had been selling large quantities of other fiber products to China since the early 1970s.

3. In dealing with China, Celanese had cultivated a reputation for meeting its commitments. A standard practice of Celanese was to be careful and specific about delivery dates, quality, terms of sale, and the like—and then to make sure it did what it said it would do. Clear understandings and reliability characterized relationships with Celanese—features that carried over into the negotiation of the joint venture—even when the Chinese preferred to postpone resolution of sensitive points.

4. Celanese is represented in China by an agent—London Export Company (LEC)—that is exceptionally competent in helping Celanese understand what is happening in China. As will be explained more fully in the next chapter, LEC can advise Celanese about actions that are realistic and acceptable. With this help, Celanese can work with Chinese organizations more smoothly and constructively.

5. Most of Celanese's international competitors produce tow only in their home countries. (Deutsche Rhodia, with a plant in Brazil, is one

exception.) In contrast, Celanese has extensive experience operating tow plants in foreign locations. It has tow plants in Belgium and Canada, and has a joint venture in Mexico. The Chinese setting, of course, differs greatly from these three countries. Nevertheless, some background with decentralized management and with operations in different cultures should help a partner understand its role in a joint venture.

For these reasons Celanese naturally was one of the potential partners that CNTC considered as it sought help in tow production. The overriding question, however, was Celanese's eagerness to cooperate in the venture—and that was unclear.

Divergent Views within Celanese about Participating in a Joint Venture

For Celanese a technology transfer to China by itself was clearly unattractive. The size of payment or royalty that the Chinese are willing to pay for technology is far below the drop in revenue that Celanese feared might result from release of the technology. Cultural differences in the concept of proprietary rights to use technical knowledge (patents), coupled with different views on the value of market positions, create such a wide gap that negotiation about transfer alone appeared futile to Celanese. Within Celanese there was wide agreement against a one-time sale of technology.

Views about other forms of cooperation differed sharply. Celanese's Far East marketing people and LEC as their advisor believed that different types of cooperation should be explored. Their belief was that one-fourth of the future world market should not be ignored; counter-proposals showing a willingness to cooperate should be made. The long-run trend toward global competition suggested that Celanese should try to maintain a presence in a market of this size.

To those holding this view, CNTC's move toward joint ventures opened the possibility of establishing such a position.

The "realists" in Celanese, on the other hand, pointed to the weakness of joint ventures—especially in China. For instance:

1. Support activities, which are beyond the control of the joint venture, frequently upset projected growth. Materials and parts from local suppliers may be unavailable or of poor quality; electric power

often fails; transportation is slow and undependable. In addition, while the number of people on the company payroll increases, the availability of skilled and motivated workers and supervisors is very tight. As a result, bringing a new joint venture up to its planned volume and income is typically delayed by several years.

2. Even when operations do reach satisfactory levels, net profits may suffer because of unexpected deductions and taxes. Contributions to an employees' welfare fund and/or a technology development fund are often required. Local transaction taxes may appear. Companies associated with rich foreign corporations are, understandably, viewed as sources of funds for urgent local needs. Money for "large" dividends to stockholders is not a high priority.

3. Then, getting foreign exchange to transfer such dividends as are declared back to a foreign parent is an additional hurdle. Arrangements made in good faith at one date may be subject to a severe financial crunch five years later.

When managers in Celanese's headquarters calculated such risks as these the probable net profit from a joint venture with CNTC over the first five years, or even ten years, was low.

Such a low estimated net profit, however, does not always kill a project. The choice of an international strategy by Celanese, as in any company, depends on the criteria—the values—that senior managers apply to various options that they have. This question of values became a dominant issue in Celanese's response in 1984 to CNTC's invitation to discuss a joint venture to produce tow in China.

One group believed that long-run market position was very important. Although hard to measure in quantitative terms, this group felt that future growth and perhaps even survival depended on having established positions in major world markets. Some current income, they believed, should be sacrificed to cultivate future opportunities. So, in keeping with this value set, they favored exploring the proposal of a joint venture with CNTC.

A second group in high positions in Celanese management believed in maximizing cash flow. Celanese had many places, both domestic and foreign, where it could make investments. And for the second group the acid test in choosing among these investments was cash.

Short-run cash gain was most prized, but future cash flows were also recognized provided that discounts were made for the length of time before the cash would be received and for the risk that projected income would not be realized. So this second group did not rule out doing business with China. Rather, for them the critical question was *when* would the net cash flow occur and what were the *odds* that various amounts would actually be received. Obviously in this sort of calculation near-term exports of tow from the United States to China are favored, whereas joint-venture profits are so delayed and uncertain that their "discounted cash value" receives little weight.

At the beginning of 1984 CNTC was pushing Celanese for a reply to its invitation to discuss a joint venture. Celanese was stalling because of its internal disagreement about what to say, while CNTC felt that it had to move ahead with its plans for local production of tow. In these circumstances the then-senior management of Celanese resolved the issue in favor of the cash flow faction. In March 1984 CNTC was told that Celanese had officially decided not to enter into discussions about a joint venture to produce tow.

The Continuing Gap

This reply from Celanese again left CNTC without an attractive way of obtaining tow. The need for a domestic source of tow as a step in modernization continued; indeed, the economic demand probably was becoming more pressing. But a structure for a sound joint venture that would help to meet this need had not yet been found.

Chapter 5

Developing a Sound Basis for Joint Action

Prospects for a joint venture with Celanese to produce tow in China appeared to end in March 1984. Celanese had said ''no'' to discussion of the subject, and CNTC was under pressure to proceed promptly to develop a local supply.

Not so. The apparent stalemate served as a spur for each side to reconsider its position. There was a common ground. The present chapter reviews the factors that led to this sharp turnaround.

Lack of Fit Between CNTC and Celanese Goals

Each potential partner had a set of goals based on its own provincial (inward) viewpoint. As noted in the preceding chapter, Celanese management was stressing cash flow from current tow sales; future expected income, while desirable, had to be discounted for delay and risk. Indeed, a chief concern about the future was protection against increasing competition. Added world capacity would only make Celanese's existing capacity more difficult to fill, and some of the plants were already partly idle.

A joint venture to build a new plant in China did not fit in with these goals of Celanese. Any investment made by Celanese would probably involve an outflow of cash—not an inflow, and the return in the form of dividends was years away and uncertain. China was admittedly seeking exports, so a new tow plant there might indeed increase competition in the only area of the world where consumption of tow was increasing.

CNTC also had its agenda based on its own circumstances. Foremost, it wanted a domestic tow plant—a good-sized one with 10,000 tons per year capacity. Acquiring such a plant via a joint venture entailed several standard requirements that the central government had set for all joint ventures. These requirements included a) the most modern technology with an output guaranteed by the foreign partner—Celanese in this case; and b) 30% of the output of the joint venture was to be exported from China, thereby generating foreign exchange to buy out the foreign partner at the termination of the joint-venture contract.

Especially the Chinese government's standard requirements were unattractive to Celanese. Guaranteeing the output of a plant located in China and dependent on local labor, energy, and materials would put Celanese at considerable risks. Furthermore, the requirement to export tow was directly counter to Celanese's desire not to increase the supply of tow on the international market. Here again, locally designed goals did not fit with the interests of the other partner.

So, if one focuses on potential sources of incompatibility it is easy to see why Celanese senior management decided that discussing a joint venture was not worth the time and expense.—But this conclusion overlooked the initiative of London Export Company (LEC).

Role of LEC in Developing Compatible Goals

Celanese and CNTC had much more in common than the preceding list of conflicts implies. The needed catalyst at this moment was someone who could help each potential partner rethink and reshape its primary objectives in a way that takes into account what the other partner wants. LEC played this vital role. Such match-making is so important to joint ventures that we should review how the role was played in the CNTC/Celanese venture.

London Export Company Strengths

Based on over thirty years of experience in China, LEC has an unusual status and reputation. Jack Perry, founder of the firm, believes that service to clients should be based on a deep appreciation of each client's needs and objectives. So, early in China's economic dealing with the West when the communist government asked LEC to help locate products and machinery it wanted to obtain in Europe, Perry found out as much as he could about the purposes such purchases were to serve. He then explored sources thoroughly and informed the Chinese about alternative ways their needs might be met. This service was a vast improvement over the then typical contacts at Canton fairs. In time, the top leaders in the government learned that they could rely on the analyses and information that LEC provided. Perry became a trusted intermediary between China and Western sources.

Jack Perry's son, Stephen, took over as chief executive of LEC in 1975. He focused on building long-term relationships in China for the firm's clients, while retaining the trading and service roles that LEC had previously developed.

LEC's commitment to informed and innovative service has led to three divisions within the company—a consulting division that advises clients on constructive ways to structure their relationships with Chinese organizations, a commodity trading division that buys and sells goods (including substantial amounts of chemicals and machinery), and a business services office in Beijing that arranges meetings, sets up conferences, gathers market data, provides business-trained interpreters, secures transportation, etc. Throughout, the aim is—not glitzy protection of visiting executives at Western-style hotels—instead, the focus is on finding actions that will be mutually beneficial to foreigners and to the Chinese.

Prior Services by LEC for Celanese

The relationship between Celanese and LEC dates back to the early 1970s. When China decided to import polyester staple fiber, LEC arranged for large purchases from Celanese. Also, as noted earlier, in 1980 when Chinese cigarette manufacturers wanted to upgrade their top brands by adding filters, LEC arranged for Celanese to sell some tow to the manufacturers, and to *give* each manufacturer a [second-hand] machine for making filter rods and to send technicians to explain how to install and use the machines. For the manufacturers, this transaction side-stepped a more difficult process of importing machinery; and for Celanese and other tow producers it opened the possibility of demand in China for tow for domestic filter cigarettes.

Each of these transactions helped to make Celanese a known, reputable supplier in China.

Initiative Taken by LEC

Often LEC learns of a need in China, but does not just accept the way the need is first specified by the Chinese user and/or the terms first stated by potential suppliers. This occurred in the first Chinese import of acetate tow, just noted.

The importation of cigarette-making machines is another example. When CNTC started to rationalize the production of cigarettes there was a great need for modern equipment that makes a uniform, well-packed product at very high speeds. Molins PLC of England, one of the two leading producers of such equipment in the world, was reluctant to sell the Chinese its then leading machines for fear that the Chinese would clone the design and then export the copies in competition with Molins. LEC was able to convince Molins that, although the Chinese might copy those specific models, Molins would benefit from having its equipment accepted as standard throughout China. Molins would then have a market for parts and a favorable position to sell its later, faster models. This has happened with Molins sales to China being many times the size of the first order.

LEC has had a somewhat similar experience with the importation of machinery to make corrugated paperboard boxes. While the specific arrangements vary widely with the product and the industry, a common feature is fostering situations that encourage future growth in demand—growth in which both the Chinese buyer and foreign seller will benefit.

Reshaping CNTC Aspirations and Criteria

When LEC told CNTC that Celanese was formally rejecting an invitation to discuss a joint venture to produce tow, it also asked CNTC for three or four months to restructure the proposal. ''Changes are occurring in top management personnel at Celanese, and a modified joint venture proposal might interest the new senior executives." Since discussions with other tow producers were moving very slowly and Celanese was potentially a good partner, CNTC agreed to try a fresh approach.

The fresh approach which LEC told CNTC would be necessary to attract Celanese included the following modifications:

1. CNTC would make Celanese a preferred supplier of tow until the new plant was on-stream. Actually this provision would not cost the Chinese anything since the price was to be the "international market price" and the volume would be what the Chinese would buy anyway. Nevertheless, the commitment posed a hurdle because the Chinese rarely made such a contract for more than one year. For Celanese this commitment substantially met the cash-flow argument.

2. More difficult was an understanding that all the output of the plant would be used within China; no exports of tow from China would be made at least in the foreseeable future. In effect, since the output of the plant would replace imports, the beneficial impact on use of foreign exchange would be about the same as exports. But in 1984 Chinese dogma was that joint ventures should lead to exports; import substitution just did not count as much. Of course, Celanese was concerned, not only about foreign exchange, but preventing Chinese exports of tow from upsetting an already over-supplied world market.

3. Management of the joint venture would be shared equally—four directors from each of the partners. Although the Chinese joint venture regulations contained a provision that contributions to registered capital would be considered in selecting directors, a 50/50 split seemed fair to the Chinese. For Celanese this arrangement would provide some protection from a change in Chinese strategy regarding exports or wider use of Celanese technology.

4. The plant would be located in Nantong where transportation was much better than the alternative locations of Xian or Jilin. This provision suited CNTC but was not popular with the Defense or Chemical Ministries.

5. CNTC would assist the joint-venture operating company to get the necessary hard currency to pay Celanese its dividends (when declared) in dollars, and also hard currency to buy back Celanese

investment at the end of the agreement fifteen years hence. CNTC is involved in several foreign trading operations, so it is in a much stronger position to arrange foreign exchange payments than a manufacturing plant in Nantong that sells all of its output within China.

To an objective outsider these modifications in the prospective joint-venture contract do not involve significant sacrifices by the Chinese. Nevertheless, for each point CNTC would have to secure agreement from several ministries or planning commissions—no small task within three months in the Chinese government. CNTC did agree to seek permission to offer these terms.

Reshaping Celanese Aspirations and Criteria

LEC also had work to do within Celanese. This involved getting a realigned management to see the attraction of a joint venture with the adjustments CNTC had been asked to make.

1. An obvious shift for Celanese would require that it give up any expectation that China could be prevented from making much of its own tow. If Celanese doesn't provide know-how some other company will. So the key question was whether Celanese wanted another world supplier—probably Eastman—to be the dominant foreign participant in tow production within the large China market.

2. Celanese's primary source of profits, however, would come from continuing sale of products to China—mostly tow but later cellulose acetate flake. These sales would come from being the preferred supplier of China's imported margin between local production and total requirements. Forecasts of growing demand indicated that a margin of imports would persist at least ten years while capacity would lag behind consumption. Significant for Celanese, the cash flow from such sales would come early, or "up front," in the overall development.

3. To deserve and maintain its position of preferred supplier, Celanese would have to perform better than potential competitors in a) helping China build and operate domestic plants, and b) supplying quality products on time at international prices. Exploitation would be out. Celanese would have to continually earn the trust that it was the best source of outside help that CNTC could find.

4. To keep the scope of CNTC activities within agreed-upon bounds, Celanese would have to exercise care that agreements were clear and specific, and it would have to select members of the board of directors who were active and informed about the Chinese situation.

As with LEC's advice to CNTC, these recommendations to Celanese were far from radical. They do call for a commitment to enter into a long-term relationship that would serve both CNTC's and Celanese's interests at the same time.

An Agreement to Negotiate is Made

The stage was set. LEC's counsel was accepted. Four months after Celanese turned down CNTC's invitation to explore a joint venture the two parties met, in July 1984, and agreed upon the basic premises on which detailed negotiations of a joint-venture contract would be based. After over two long years of probing and learning a common ground was quickly defined.

Actually the Celanese team had to return to the United States to get official approval from the senior management of Celanese, and other checks were made. So it was October before the formal agreement to negotiate was settled. But a basic "meeting of the minds" occurred at that first joint session in July.

Two major points, as well as many minor ones, had been added by October. Celanese proposed that some of its idle equipment in the United States be reconditioned for use in the new plant. This reduced the necessary capital investment. So an added feature of the final joint-venture proposal was a bargain price!

Also, Celanese noted that the very specific engineering studies needed for the technology-transfer agreement, work on the joint feasibility study, and drafting of the final contract all involved substantial expense and time of key people. Consequently, at Celanese's request, the division of CNTC that was in charge of the Nantong location (the Jiangsu Tobacco Company) agreed to negotiate only with Celanese until an agreement was reached or abandoned. This exclusive negotiation was unusual. The standard pattern recommended by the State Council is to secure three competing proposals for each major contract. CNTC felt that it had already met this requirement in its prior discussions with other world cigarette manufacturers. Also the contract about to be negotiated was to be much more specific than is usually the case. So exclusive negotiation was added to the basic premises.

The prolonged process of negotiating the actual joint-venture contract is the grist of Part II of this report. Before turning to that subject in the next chapter, we will take a second look at the series of events leading up to the agreement to negotiate—seeking implied guidelines that may be useful to other companies that are trying to get a joint-venture opportunity into sharper focus.

Chapter 6

Conclusion of Part I—Developing a Workable Conception of the Joint Venture

Each joint venture is a tailor-made organization. Because it has two or more sponsoring companies—each with its own objectives—a joint venture is fragile. So, the benefits of joint action must be strong, and the guidelines for cooperating must be clear, if their joint venture is to survive in a modern, turbulent environment.

The present case study indicates that the probability of building a strong joint venture is greatly increased when the basic concepts—the underlying premises—of the venture are clarified before more detailed negotiations begin. Agreement among the partners, and other people or organizations whose support is essential, regarding a workable framework for the new child gives focus to the more specific planning. Without such a framework detailed analysis will be confused and probably futile.

The preceding chapters in Part I describe how such a workable conception of the CNTC/Celanese joint venture evolved over a period of years. To conclude Part I, a list of particularly helpful events or actions are singled out as possible guidelines for managers who will be creating future joint ventures in China.

Implied Guidelines for Future Designers of Joint Ventures

Several features contributed strongly to getting the CNTC and Celanese joint venture negotiations launched successfully. Similar devices will not fit exactly to other formative stages. Nevertheless, this one experience does suggest that something like the following features might be very beneficial in a wide range of joint venture initiations.

1. *Develop a workable conception first.* Agreement on the following points is needed as a base for more detailed planning:
   a. the benefits expected from the cooperative activity;
   b. the nature, approximate size and timing of each partner's contributions;
   c. constraints on each partner and on the new operating company which each partner will insist on;
   d. division among partners of the net output of the new operating company;
   e. provision for managing the operating company and for terminating it.

Such a "structure of the deal" will serve as the basic premises around which the more specific plans will be negotiated. The requirement that the conception be workable means that the contemplated joint activities are realistic in the environment, and that partners will be able to make their contributions. Some uncertainty about workability is unavoidable, of course; but the sources and magnitude of future difficulties should be recognized and be tolerable by each partner.

An aspect of this approach to developing a joint venture is that detailed planning of one or two parts—such as a factory design or marketing channels—should not start until the overall concept is settled. Premature detailed planning is likely to be a waste of effort because the scope of activities may change or disagreement on some key feature may kill the whole idea. CNTC wisely postponed specific plant designing until a clear meeting of minds with a partner was achieved.

2. *Recognize that the needs of both partners must be well served.* Many of the regulations and other guides for designing a joint venture

focus on self-protection. The aim of such guidelines is to assure that the other partner does not take undue advantage by withholding valuable inputs or gaining most of the benefits. Reflecting a long history of dealing with foreigners, the Chinese fear exploitation; and regulations include provisions which are intended to protect the People's Republic of China against such abuse in the future.

At the same time, stories are common about the Chinese expecting investments, access to proprietary know-how, and other inputs from a foreign partner—with only the prospect of quite uncertain returns several years later. The foreign partner fears that efforts on his part will get lost in a complex and ambiguous Chinese business system. So the foreign partner is also concerned about being out-maneuvered.

If early negotiations get bogged down with each partner trying only to protect his own interests, the chances of success are small. Instead, each partner must also look for ways that will benefit the other partner. The joint venture must continue to be strongly attractive to both partners. Unless mutual benefits prevail, the inevitable frictions that come with mixing two cultures will cause one or both partners to stop cooperating.

The present study did not gather data on CNTC's negotiations with other potential partners in tow production. The indirect information that we picked up, however, suggests that CNTC's discussions with Daicel, Eastman, and Deutsche Rhodia did not reach a mutual agreement at least partly because both sides kept focusing on their own interests. A way *both* sides might benefit never took clear shape.

3. *Consider using a catalyst.* As explained in the preceding chapter, an agreement by CNTC and Celanese even to discuss a joint venture was almost missed. LEC (London Export Company) became the necessary catalyst. And LEC succeeded by getting each side to think about ways that the joint venture might be made more attractive to the other partner.

An intermediary who understands the viewpoints of both potential partners may be more creative than either partner acting alone. He is less immersed in conventional practices and freer to think about different arrangements. As the role of an investment banker in the United States indicates, "restructuring" opens up new ways to satisfy particular needs.

4. *Get long-run commitment from top management to a joint venture in China.* Starting a joint venture is more than a single transaction.

Instead, it presumes a relationship lasting ten to twenty or more years. During this period turbulence in the country and the company of each partner will modify their interest in the joint venture. Unless senior managers in each company have a belief that doing business cooperatively in China is a wise strategy, the joint venture is likely to fall apart when the first need for modification arises.

The present executives of Celanese recognized the need for such a commitment. The former senior management, however, doubted that trying to conduct business within China was worth the aggravation and expense; so they did not want to start talking about a joint venture. In contrast, the present executives believe that a world supplier of tow, such as Celanese, should be actively involved in the quarter of the world market existing in China; so they clearly supported the joint venture.

A commitment to doing business in China calls for at least one or two senior managers being up-to-date on basic developments in that country. This takes senior managers' time to make occasional visits and to keep informed. Sound decisions as the local venture evolves cannot be based only on historical financial results. Moreover, the commitment is based on a belief that China is important to the company now and in the future.

On the Chinese side, commitment has similar dimensions. Senior Chinese managers need to develop familiarity with the global industry of which they are a part. Also, they need a belief that working cooperatively with foreign companies will be good for the long-run development of China. Note that this implies a shift in attitude from an idea current in China a decade ago—that China could develop in substantial isolation from the outside world if it just had Western technology.

Briefly, then, this guideline says that foreign/Chinese joint ventures should be treated as important long-term commitments by both parents. In some circumstances short-term deals may be warranted. But building and sustaining a good joint venture takes so much effort that it is warranted only when both partners believe that long-run cooperation will be mutually beneficial.

5. *Seek a way to get coordinated action in China.* Governing a large nation like China is inevitably complicated. And because the Chinese government is going through rapid stages of development, uncertainty is added to the complexity. One result is that approvals necessary to design and operate a joint venture keep changing. Securing capital

grants, foreign exchange, qualified personnel, dependable tax treatment, material quotas, and similar support is not only difficult; actions taken by different departments may be inconsistent.

The CNTC/Celanese joint venture was greatly facilitated by the formulation of CNTC just as the thrust to build a major tow plant got underway. Designed as an industry monopoly, CNTC had within its own organization many of the activities that had to be coordinated to put together a viable joint venture. Moreover, CNTC's status of reporting directly to the State Council helped to obtain cooperation from outside ministries. Without this unusual way for securing coordination, creation of NCFC (Nantong Cellulose Fibers Company) and construction of the tow plant would have been long delayed.

New joint ventures will confront similar difficulties, and few will have a national monopoly organization to short-circuit bureaucratic arguments. Consequently, some other innovative ways to secure coordination will be needed.

6. *Respond to timing opportunities*. China's economic development is very dynamic. The goals are ambitious; new regulations are introduced every few years; the emphasis shifts as current needs change; significant learning occurs at all levels. One aspect of this dynamism is that the role which joint ventures are expected to play in various segments of the economy keeps changing. This means that a venture which was unattractive at one time may become attractive a short time later.

Of course, foreign companies also change in their directions of development and their available resources. Views about opportunities and requirements for global competition lead to revisions of company strategies. If thrusts in one direction are blocked a company may commit resources, perhaps irrevocably, to an alternative course of action.

Such double variability—in the Chinese situation and in foreign company interests—opens and closes "windows of opportunity." The *time* that an effort is made may have as much to do with its success as a specific feature of a proposal.

Timing was crucial, for example, in the negotiation of the CNTC/Celanese tow joint venture. On the CNTC side, China's development from an open-door policy through attempts to buy technology to accepting and encouraging joint ventures was taking place during the time period covered in Part I of our report. Also, the move to a national tobacco monopoly and the formation of CNTC significantly affected the opportunity for workable joint ventures to produce tow in China.

Likewise, Celanese's view of global competition and its resulting shift in policy regarding foreign involvements sharply altered Celanese interest in a joint venture. Fortunately, the changes in both Celanese and China took place at about the same time. In 1983 neither partner was prepared to enter into the agreement that eventually emerged. And a delay to 1985 by either partner might have been too late. The window of opportunity was in 1984.

Sound joint ventures often arise from being ready to move at the right moment.

*   *   *

The six guidelines sketched above apply to equity joint ventures. At least in creating the NCFC joint venture, each was crucial. If these guidelines cannot be met to a substantial degree, then a simpler sort of joint effort—such as sale of technology or a production contract—probably would have a better chance of success.

Part II

Turning Agreement on Key Features Into A Clear Joint Venture Contract

An agreement "in principle" is far fom a plan of action. In the Nantong Cellulose Fibers Company joint venture case, the Chinese expected this decision elaboration process to take about six months. Actually it took more than two years of negotiation before the joint venture contract was signed.

In Part II we explore why reaching a clear agreement took so much time, and what was accomplished in these prolonged discussions.

Significantly, the NCFC negotiations were not delayed by sharp controversy—as often arises in joint venture discussions. The key features of the final contract were the same points agreed to at the beginning of negotiations in July-October of 1984. Instead, most of the time was consumed in thinking through just what activities would be necessary to make the joint venture a practical, productive organization; in deciding who would provide what resources, and how the enterprise would be managed; and in securing approvals of these plans.

Reaching a sound foreign joint venture agreement in China involves more planning and learning, by both partners, than is typical for Western joint ventures.

a. While any foreign joint venture calls for a linking of cultures, such reconciliation is extensive when a Western and Chinese organization join forces. The language, institutions, and business customs of the two partners will differ. To avoid misunderstandings special effort is needed to assure that both parties have similar conceptions in their minds. And where local practices (e.g., accounting or methods of competition) differ, a choice of which to follow is necessary. In contrast, a domestic joint venture is built on a common language and business setting.

b. Moreover, the newness of the use of joint ventures in the Chinese economic system adds to the task of reaching mutual understanding. People in various government ministries and regions do not yet have a common recognition of the self-reliance and powers of a joint venture. And efforts to "decentralize" business planning are still being refined. This unsettled setting does not mean that specific agreements for a particular joint venture cannot be made; rather, more dicussion is needed to arrive at a clear agreement.

c. Despite such strange and unsettled conditions, the two partners in the NCFC venture sought clarity in their agreement. Rarely will a troublesome issue become easier to resolve by postponing it. Moreover, by confronting problems in the formative period the general concepts of the venture can be tested for their practicality. So the NCFC partners made minimum use of "We will consider that later," even though pursuing clarity did delay signing a contract.

A different sort of hurdle is the overlapping of documents that are required for approval of a joint venture in China. Key documents involved in the formation of NCFC included:

- Joint feasibility study.
- Joint venture contract.
- Technology transfer contract, which was incorporated as a part of the joint venture contract.
- Equipment investment principles—including lists of kinds of equipment to be supplied by each party to the joint venture contract.
- Articles of association, based on the joint venture contract.

Also, a variety of permits at the municipal and provincial levels were necessary.

Although these documents can be mutually supporting, trouble arises because regulations surrounding them were written for quite different purposes. A one-time purchase of technology, for instance, calls for safeguards that do not suit a long-run cooperation.

Negotiating an agreement in the general setting just noted calls for an unusual amount of effort and persistence. The problems, and how they were met for NCFC, are described in the following chapters:

Chapter 7

People in the Negotiating Process

Joint venture agreements are made by people—individuals with their own values, strengths, loyalties, and biases. The more pioneering and unprecedented the agreement, the greater is the influence of particular persons who do the negotiating. So, to understand how the fledgling Nantong Cellulose Fibers Company took the form it did, we need to describe the key participants who negotiated the joint venture contract.

The people who had a distinctive impact on the CNTC-Celanese negotiation will be identified in terms of:

    a. Status: who deals with whom
    b. Characteristics of top negotiators
    c. Crucial role of advisors
    d. Building consensus

Status: Who Deals with Whom

The selection of negotiators in this case was simplified by the informal agreement that was so quickly made between CNTC and Celanese. Earlier other possibilities existed. The first domestic production of tow might have been done by the Ministry of Light Industry, the Ministry of Chemical Production, or the Defense Ministry; the plant location might have been at Jilin or Xian. In fact, CNTC seized the initiative for a plant to be located at Nantong.

Even within these organizational and geographic constraints there were several options for where the negotiations would be centered in the economic structure. A variety of factors needed to be embraced in the joint venture agreement. Local issues of employment, housing, power and water supply, and air pollution were best known in Nantong itself. On the other hand, the allocation of tow to various cigarette plants and the obtaining of foreign exchange for imports, for example, had to be handled on a national level at Beijing.

Status also was a consideration. Officials of CNTC preferred not to deal with field personnel of a subsidiary of Celanese; and Celanese had a comparable concern. Both authority and time of very busy people were at stake.

This question of who deals with whom was resolved by designating the specific organization units that would become the legal partners in the joint venture. For CNTC (the recently formed China National Tobacco Company) its regional operating unit, Jiangsu Tobacco Company, was to be the active partner—Jiangsu being the povince in which Nantong is located. For Celanese (U.S.) its subsidiary, Celanese Fibers Operations, Ltd., was to be the active partner. With this set-up, a senior official of each partner became the top negotiator—Xu Li-Yu, General Manager of the Jiangsu Tobacco Company and Robert L. Stultz, Vice President of Celanese Fibers Operations, Ltd.

Note that each negotiator had direct access to his large parent company whose continuing support was crucial. And, each negotiator was relatively close to actual operations in his respective organization. This linking relationship, both up and down, proved to be very valuable in developing a coordinated plan for the new joint venture. Other prospective joint ventures in China which are tied most closely either to the top of the managerial pyramid or to the operating level have trouble devising a workable plan of action.

Characteristics of Top Negotiators

Celanese was represented by an unusually qualified team. Stultz, who holds an engineering degree, had long experience as an international marketing vice president for Celanese. He was put in charge of developing the tow business in China as a capstone project prior to his retirement. Stephen Perry of London Export Company says, "Bob Stultz is a rare ingredient. He is a senior, very experienced manager who understands a lot about production. I've seen him in action and his range of skills is very broad—the sort of person who could run different sorts of businesses. Most companies put people on the China exercise who lack Bob's diversity of skills. He doesn't get deflected by secondary issues; instead, he'll push those to one side and keep pursuing his main objective aggressively but very pleasantly. He's positive, persistent, and polite."

This high regard for Stultz is shared by Celanese top managers who gave him full charge of the negotiation with CNTC and authority to speak for the company. Incidentally, assigning a person of Stultz's stature sent a signal to the Chinese about Celanese's serious interest in the joint venture project.

A second key person in the negotiations was Katy Coe. The daughter of American parents, she grew up in China. She is not only bi-lingual but bi-cultural. And having worked ten years for London Export Company she is very knowledgeable about Chinese government and business practices.

Coe really performed a double role. In addition to interpreting for Stultz, she served as a skilled mediator between the Americans and the Chinese. She could explain the background and implications of a Chinese proposal to the Americans, and vice versa. She frequently provided an informal communication link, and often injected her own suggestions for ways to overcome rough terrain. Cordial and constructive, Coe was respected by both the Chinese and the Americans.

Xu Li-Yu brought a different kind of skill to the negotiations. Developing a multi-million yuan tow business in a provincial city of China was, of course, a novel experience for a wide range of people that would be affected. And Xu himself was not presumed to be an expert in plant construction or operations. Rather, his main contribution was knowing who at the local level and at the national level should be consulted, obtaining their viewpoints, and developing a consensus on various issues. Two key people at the national level were Hu Gong Pu and Jin Maoxian of CNTC. In China especially such consensus-building is an essential step in launching a new joint venture.

Crucial Roles of Advisors

The two central negotiators just described needed technical advice, of course. Stultz could and did frequently call on Celanese's technical staff of engineers, lawyers, etc. He also employed an outside engineering firm (CRS Sirrine) to do the substantial task of planning and preparing specifications for the "battery limits" section of the new plant for which Celanese was responsible.

These relationships among the Americans followed well established patterns based on previous projects. The only new dimension was applying the work to the Chinese setting. This transition to China did pose some problems of coordination with Xu's advisors, as will be discussed in Chapters 8 and 10. However, at no time was there question about the quality or timeliness of the advice received.

Xu likewise sought technical advice. But here the relationship to Xu differed from Stultz's relations with his advisors. Most of Xu's advisors came from organizations affiliated with a different ministry.

We believe that the Chinese technical advisors apparently felt more loyalty to their home ministry than to the progress of the project. Rather than viewing their work as helping the user (customer) of the advice, they seemed to feel that they had been given a separate task which could be performed as and when it fitted into their schedule. Contributing to this independent attitude was a strong tendency to follow in detail any generalized written instructions from Beijing; the technical advisors appeared to be more interested in avoiding any confrontation with centralized reviewing and approving agencies than with the needs of the joint venture.

An early issue in the negotiations was which engineering design institute would serve Jiangsu Tobacco Company (JTC) on technology and plant design matters. The first Engineering Design Institute selected by JTC soon made it clear that it would favor a technology which differed in part from Celanese technology. The Institute took this position even though Celanese had been selected for detailed negotiations partly because its plants were recognized as among the best in the world.

In view of the independent attitude common among technical institutes—noted above—this disagreement regarding technology promised to be a serious stumbling block throughout the negotiations. Also, there was some disagreement about the service charge. Even so, a switch in JTC's technology advisors was made only after Stultz's strong insistence.

This incident illustrates that the relationships in China between general managers and the experts who "advise" them may differ sharply from such relationships in the United States.

Building Consensus

The setting for negotiations, outlined above, created a favorable stage. Representatives of the specific units selected to be partners (not lawyers or brokers) became the head negotiators. And these partners were well placed to link concrete operating problems with broad strategic and financial goals of their respective parents. The individuals in these roles had skills, status, and commitment to envisage a new company that would be viable. Good technical advice was available— although some of the Chinese advisors felt little commitment to getting the Nantong joint venture launched promptly.

In addition to such competent negotiating teams, three features of the negotiating process were particularly helpful in arriving at a consensus about the joint venture contract.

a. *Single negotiation*

A condition requested by Celanese before starting on discussions of a specific joint venture agreement was that its counterpart—Jiangsu Tobacco Company—negotiate only with Celanese until an agreement was reached or the cooperative project definitely abandoned by either of the parties. In other words, concurrent negotiations with a competitor were ruled out. The reasons for this arrangement included:

1. The expenses of preparing a joint venture agreement are substantial, especially when the planning is to be carried down to layouts and equipment specifications. (In fact, Celanese spent over four million dollars before the agreement was signed.) Celanese was reluctant to make this investment unless the prospects for reaching agreement were high.

2. Effective plans for cooperation needed to be based on the best data available, and some of this information was confidential. Celanese, and also JTC, did not want to present confidential data in a situation where competitors were likely to learn about it.

3. By no means least was an expectation by everyone involved that this venture would soon be in operation. Attention then shifted from jockeying for narrow gains toward finding ways that would help the new company (NCFC) become most effective. Negotiations tended to shift from a win-lose viewpoint to a win-win attitude.

JTC and Celanese did observe this concentrated negotiation agreement throughout the planning period.

Celanese's understanding with CNTC was not so restrictive. Here the agreement was only that CNTC would not sign a tow production agreement with another company without talking to Celanese. In fact, CNTC did not enter into formal negotiations with any other company during this period. Acting alone and rather late, a Celanese competitor did prepare—with assistance of another Engineering Design Institute— a feasibility study for a joint venture at the Nantong site. This study was available to the State Planning Commission at the same time that the JTC-Celanese feasibility study was being reviewed. Thus CNTC and the Planning Commission did have an alternative plan with which to compare the joint study. However, this plan did not represent mutual agreement with a Chinese partner.

b. *No surprises*

A quite different aspect of building consensus is the way agendas for negotiating sessions were formed. Some of the slick U.S. books on negotiating recommend keeping your "opponent" off-balance by unexpectedly introducing new information or new proposals. In China this is a poor tactic. At least in the JTC-Celanese negotiations, "No surprises" worked well.

For instance, in advance of a scheduled discussion, and certainly by the preceding evening, an intermediary (usually Coe) informed the chief Chinese spokesman of an issue, proposal, or important information that the U.S. negotiator wished to introduce at the next discussion. The Chinese negotiators likewise sent messages. On some matters the receiver of such a message might ask for time to prepare a response, and later communicate whether or not the proposal would be acceptable. For quite important or delicate topics the two top negotiators might meet informally to chart a course for the next session. Katy Coe was especially adept at uncovering what was really at stake and suggesting approaches to exploration of issues. If unusual solutions were involved, time for LEC to help explain and gain support within partners' organizations might be needed before the proposal was put on the agenda.

The benefits of such exchanges were 1) avoiding embarrassment at more public discussions, 2) providing each negotiator time to consult his advisors in private and/or to consult with a third party who might be affected, and 3) encouraging the thoughtful devising of acceptable courses of action. In other words, this "no surprises at public meetings" is a practice that tends to avoid polarization of viewpoints; instead, it is a face-saving way to build consensus.

c. *Memorandum of agreement*

Creating a consensus was also aided by the use of "memorandum of agreement." Often at the close of a set of negotiating meetings, Xu and Stultz prepared and signed a summary statement of the points on which agreement had been reached during the preceding two or three days.

These memorandums were valuable for several reasons:

1. The negotiations took place at meetings, about a month apart, for a period of over two years. During that length of time memories can become clouded. Without a written statement, each person relies on a selective memory of what actually took place; time may be consumed recalling agreements, or issues previously settled may be reopened for debate.

2. A joint venture agreement is (or should be) an *integrated* plan. For example, agreement on product specifications becomes a premise for selection of equipment; equipment selection affects financing plans, etc. It is important, of course, that all those engaged in planning use the same premises. In the JTC-Celanese negotiations memorandums of agreement served as anchor points in achieving such integrated planning.

3. Memorandums of agreement also encourage *long-range* planning. The Nantong joint venture and the companies that created it are all taking actions now that they believe will provide strengths ten and twenty years hence. Because this long-range planning is filled with uncertainties, any device that clarifies and tends to stabilize some parts of the near-term setting also provides a better base for longer-term projections.

The memorandums of agreement are part of the mental process that make long-range planning possible. Instead of approaching every issue as a continuing chain of short-term deals always open for renewed bargaining—as is common in the Middle East and to a lesser extent in China—some commitments are stabilized. Perhaps revisions may become necessary, but a foundation is established for the foreseeable future.

Developing agreement on the many facets of a joint venture contract calls for numerous exchanges of proposals, information, wording, and other give-and-take. From all this exchange an integrated consensus about the final provisions to put into the contract must be built. The three practices just described—single negotiations, no surprises, and memorandums of agreement—greatly aided the negotiators of the Nantong Cellulose Fibers Company contract in reaching such a consensus.

Conclusion: Guidelines Suggested

The experience reported in this chapter suggests several guides for future negotiators of joint ventures in China:

1. Negotiations will proceed faster and are more likely to result in a practical plan when the company representative a) is an executive with general management experience, b) is authorized to commit his company, c) has time to sit through a series of meetings, and d) is patient, persistent, and polite.

2. Several levels of administration should have direct inputs to the negotiations early enough to receive careful consideration. For instance, in the NCFC planning this meant that *both* national headquarters of CNTC and officials in the city of Nantong where the plant was to be located indicated what was practical from their respective points of view while the joint venture contract was still in a formative stage.

3. Factors to weigh when selecting technical advisors should include—in addition to technical competence and availability—a primary desire to serve the best interests of the new company being formed.

4. To facilitate coming to an agreement on a specific, practical, integrated plan for the new venture—after the prospective partners have agreed upon a basic design—a single negotiation is desirable. Also a "no surprises" procedure, and the use of interim "memorandums of agreement" help to reach a coordinated consensus.

All of these points will be further illustrated in the next four chapters.

Chapter 8

Agreeing On Plant Technology

Plant technology to produce cellulose acetate tow was the crucial core around which the Nantong Cellulose Fibers Company was built. The Chinese wanted a physical process that Celanese could provide. Surprisingly, months of negotiation were used in moving from this simple proposition to specific plans for a tow plant in Nantong—not to mention another year for agreeing on the characteristics of the joint venture that was to construct and operate the plant.

The present chapter focuses on achieving agreement on just the plans for the plant. Other important features of the joint venture are described in following chapters.

The technical aspects of planning the Nantong plant posed no major problems. Celanese engineers were familiar with the production of tow, and Chinese engineering firms were familiar with equipment and buildings necessary for support services. Instead, difficulties arose in shifting from a simple purchase of technology to the use of technology by a joint venture. At least in 1984–85, the Chinese engineers were unprepared to distinguish between bargaining and safeguards involved in the purchase of technology compared with a cooperative approach suited to a joint venture. Also, questions arose over how specific joint venture planning should be. More time was spent on learning what was appropriate for a foreign joint venture than on actual plant design.

Examples of those viewpoint issues will be presented in the following sections:

Using P.R.C. instructions for planning

Confronting rather than deferring unresolved issues

Local versus foreign planning

Zeal of independent advisors

Output guarantees

Timing of coordination

Using P.R.C. Instructions for Planning

Agreements between foreign companies and companies within the People's Republic of China were relatively new in the 1980s. Indeed the recognition of separate, limited liability companies was new. So, the Chinese government had issued regulations and guidelines on what would be acceptable. The two prospective NCFC partners decided to conform to these instructions if it was feasible for them to do so. Even the wording in written contracts followed the existing patterns to the extent that they fit the new venture.

As we shall note, such reliance on existing patterns speeded up negotiations and government approval on some points, but it also created new hurdles when exceptions were necessary. Conformity has its price.

Guidelines for three kinds of documents were used—a) feasibility studies of potential joint ventures, b) technology transfer contracts, and c) joint venture contracts. These instruments are very briefly described in Exhibit 8-1. Although these instruments serve different purposes there is a lot of overlap in their contents.

To deal with this overlap the NCFC negotiators assumed that agreement on the technology to be used would come first. That agreement would then be a part of the joint feasibility study. And the joint venture contract, even broader in scope than the feasibility study, would incorporate the main points of both the technology transfer and feasibility documents. The final outcome is a single, comprehensive, and integrated agreement—not three separate agreements prepared at different times by different people.

This arrangement sounds simple. In practice, the catch was that the Chinese government's standard instructions to Chinese negotiators

EXHIBIT 8-1
Brief Descriptions of Basic Documents

Joint Feasibility Study

A report describing a proposed joint venture in China by a foreign company and a Chinese enterprise, showing the benefits and costs anticipated. Topics covered in such a report usually include: products and services to be produced, prospective markets and competition, selling prices, foreign exchange that will be generated, sources of raw materials and utilities, operating costs, profit projections, local and foreign personnel needed—and expenses of foreign personnel, a materials balance sheet, a financial balance sheet, total investment required, advantages of foreign participation. The report goes to the State Planning Commission for approval of a place for the joint venture project in China's overall economic development program.

Technology Transfer Contract

Contains a description of a state-of-the-art technology being supplied by a foreign company to a Chinese enterprise—including documentation, licenses, training of personnel, subsequent technical exchanges, and guarantees. Also covers the period and scope of use of the technology, and the terms of payment. To prevent exploitation, the Chinese government has a tough set of conditions which must be met before approval of a contract is granted.

Joint Venture Contract

Contract between a foreign company and a Chinese enterprise to cooperate in forming a limited liability company in China. Special legislation permitting such joint ventures is new because for many years self-governed, stockholder-owned corporations have been illegal in the People's Republic of China. Regulations governing such joint ventures were still being refined at the time of this study. A typical joint venture agreement includes provisions for: type and scope of business, sources of capital, board of directors and business management office, technology transfer, purchase of plant and raw materials, personnel management and union organization, sales of products and treatment of foreign exchange, taxes and audit, special funds and dividends, dissolution of the company.

were written separately, at different dates, and with different aims. To prepare a single integrated agreement, the NCFC negotiators had to develop a workable reconciliation—and then hope that Beijing reviewers would recognize a need for some variations from standard instructions.

Confronting Rather Than Deferring Unresolved Issues

Although the documents required for government approval covered many topics they stopped far short of plans that could be turned over to construction contractors for execution. CFO (Celanese Fibers Operations) felt that such a cut-off level in the planning left too much room for misunderstandings; also such condensed planning had to rely on estimates of costs and construction time which could deviate widely from actual costs and completion dates.

So from the beginning of negotiations CFO insisted that the final joint venture contract be based on specific plans for the plant. The planning was to move through several steps:

Product specifications and plant capacity

Steps in the production process and auxiliary services needed

Preliminary engineering designs for each step and service

Consolidated engineering designs and estimated costs to be used in seeking government approvals

Equipment specifications, layouts, architectural drawings, and related documents adequate for letting contracts

Such planning is more detailed than is common in most joint venture contracts, certainly those in China. Nevertheless, the Nantong plant was to be the dominating core of the NCFC operations, and both JTC and CFO believed that any questions about its design should be settled sooner rather than later.

This insistence on full planning was typical of CFO's approach to the entire joint venture contract. All sorts of issues were to be faced squarely and promptly rather than put off; by doing so uncertainty was reduced and mutual agreements were devised before problems became crises.

Local versus Foreign Planning

In addition to selecting a sequence for building up the content of the joint venture agreement, just noted, the negotiators had to decide *who* would prepare detailed plans for joint review and approval.

The information needed to prepare specific plans for the proposed plant was available in dispersed locations—primarily Nantong, Nanjing, Beijing, and Shanghai in China; and Charlotte and Celanese tow plant sites in the United States. No single person or engineering firm had practical access to all this information. Nevertheless, an integrated plan for the plant was essential.

A basic division of the detailed planning task was agreed upon early in the negotiations. Celanese was responsible for preparation of specific engineering design documents for the conversion of raw materials into tow ready for shipment; these are operations within the "battery limits" section of the plant. JTC was responsible for preparation of specific engineering design documents for all auxiliary operations outside the battery limits; these operations include the processing and supply of steam, electricity, process and cooling water, compressed air, and nitrogen. In addition, JTC was responsible for civil and architectural designs for buildings, road, storage and shipping facilities, and the like throughout the entire plant.

To coordinate the plans prepared by CFO and by JTC, each partner was to review the plans prepared by the other partner at major steps. In addition, it was understood that less formal exchanges were to take place frequently.

In practice, this planning procedure was complicated by heavy reliance on outside engineering institutes or firms for advice and documentation. JTC especially had no previous experience with a large chemical processing plant and had to depend for advice from an industry engineering institute which we shall call IEI. Also the timing of the detail work on documentation had to be coordinated with other plans for the joint venture.

The priorities of the consultants and the negotiators differed, resulting in loss of time, as will soon be illustrated.

Several hurdles arose relating just to the physical technology—even though Celanese was selected as a prospective partner because of its expert knowledge about production of tow. Some of these problems are likely to arise in other joint ventures, so a brief description is given here.

Zeal of Independent Advisors

Between July 1984 when Celanese first talked with CNTC about the possibility of a joint venture and February 1985 when Chinese officials inspected Celanese plants in the United States, rapid progress on planning the NCFC company had been made. Then, after limited discussions with the Nantong Design Institute, IEI became JTC's technical advisor. And IEI questioning about operations within the battery limits went on and on for six months, delaying the entire project for at least five months! This slowdown was surprising in view of CNTC's desire to get the tow plant built promptly and Celanese's recognized expertise in tow production technology.

Several factors contributed to the delay:

a. IEI was especially anxious to be sure that it could defend its recommendations. It had been chosen to replace the Nantong Design Institute and a challenge on technical grounds was not unlikely. Even when IEI's local representatives might feel convinced, their superiors sent them back for more data. So the same issues were raised over and over, and Celanese engineers gave the same answers over and over.

It is true that Stultz frankly held back some know-how features on the grounds that if all technological skill was revealed prior to an agreement the transfer would have already occurred. Actually, such knowledge about the mystique of the process was unnecessary to an evaluation of how well the process worked.

b. Probably more troublesome was IEI's reliance on Beijing standard guidelines for negotiation of Technology Purchase Contracts. These guidelines had two very serious drawbacks for the CFO/JTC negotiations.

1. The guidelines were prepared for a single transfer, not for a continuing cooperative venture. They seemed to assume that the provider of the technology would try to exploit the Chinese. And to prevent exploitation, a wide array of information (often highly confidential from the foreign company's viewpoint) had to be obtained before the project would be approved. Many of these questions did not relate to a continuing joint venture like NCFC, yet IEI wanted them answered.

2. In addition to the publicly known guidelines for Technology Transfers, Chinese negotiators had internal (though published in a "little green book") rules that they were obliged to follow in the negotiations—again prepared for Technology Purchase Contracts. As negotiations dragged on for several months, the existence of the "little green books" could not be denied. CFO's position was that since these guidelines were in effect Chinese

law—and CFO personnel were committed to obey Chinese law—
CFO was entitled to be informed of the law which its people were
expected to honor. Chinese representatives maintained to the end
that the books were internal documents. In the CFO/JTC negotiations at least, debating unstated issues consumed a lot of time.

3. The Chinese were reluctant to ask an influential body to modify
its actions even when such actions were poorly suited to a specific
situation. In the present case, JTC permitted its advisor IEI to
prolong the questioning unduly. Similarly, IEI was clearly unwilling to tell the authorities in Beijing that some parts of the
Technology Purchase Contract guidelines did not fit a joint venture negotiation.

So, professional pride, poorly suited and sometimes secret government guidelines, and culture-based reluctance to challenge accepted
roles all combined to delay a foregone agreement.

Output Guarantees

Another serious obstacle to technology transfer agreements is Chinese insistence that the provider of the technology guarantee its
performance in China. The typical objection by the foreign provider is
that he has no control over many of the conditions—labor, quality
control, and the like—in the Chinese application of the technology.
Consequently, a process that works well in, say, the United States
may be less effective in China through no fault of the supplier of the
technology.

CFO and JTC sidestepped this problem by also stating quality
standards for the inputs entering the production process within the
battery limits from other parts of the plant—in addition to the outputs.
Recall that CFO was to prepare the engineering design and documentation (and watch over the installation) of equipment within the battery
limits, whereas JTC was to prepare the engineering design and documentation (and supervise the installation) of all auxiliary equipment
outside the battery limits. Thus, JTC is obliged to ensure that the
equipment it is providing to the joint venture operate up to explicit
standards if CFO is to be held to its guarantees of the technology and
equipment that it is providing. Both CFO and JTC must work together
to achieve the guaranteed output.

Writing the specific standards for outputs and inputs was not simple.

Key factors had to be identified and measurements defined. For example, output standards deal with tow properties, with production rates for specific sizes of tow, and with consumption amounts of main raw materials. The tow properties include filament denier, total denier, moisture, residual acetone, breaking strength, color, and the like. With these standards, "acceptable quality" has real meaning.

Input standards were also sharply defined. Examples include pressure, temperature, and purity specifications for steam, process water, cooling tower water, compressed air, electricity, and other utilities. Such specifications had to be maintained continuously during a 72-hour test run while CFO's guaranteed performance was being established.

Once such specific standards were developed, Celanese was willing to guarantee its technology because the conditions in which that technology would be used were predictable and reliable. Note that a) Celanese reviewed and approved the designs (and technical staffing) of auxiliary services at the plant. b) The inputs of steam, water, electricity, etc. had to be maintained at standards like those in U.S. plants. c) More broadly, Celanese shared in the management of the joint venture that used the technology.

The Chinese standard requirements for a Technology Transfer Contract are written to protect the Chinese user from exploitation. Nevertheless, Celanese was able, through patient and persistent negotiation and insistence on a joint venture relationship, to create a more balanced approach. Both the provider and the user of the technology must work together to utilize the technology effectively.

Also noteworthy, the quite specific input and output standards that were developed for a practical guarantee have a continuing benefit. They can be used also as guides for efficient operation of the plant year after year.

Timing of Coordination

With two separate groups—JTC with its advisors and CFO with its advisors—designing a large complex plant, coordination of the effort was crucial. Obviously, steam from the three coal-fired boilers had to arrive at the battery limits at the right place and time in order to ensure the production of specification grade product. And similarly with other interdependencies, such as electricity, cooling water, compressed air, etc.

In the early planning stages, explicit procedures for JTC to review CFO plans—and vice versa—were established. (See Exhibit 8-2.) During the discussions of processing technology, each of the engineering groups knew what the other group was thinking. The exchange of information took place early when plans were still being developed; at this stage adjustments necessary for the plans to fit together could be made easily.

In contrast, during the later stages when the preliminary designs were being detailed and construction drawings being prepared, coordination between the two planning groups was left to informal contacts. Only after the detailed plans were completed was an explicit merging called for.

CFO had assumed that engineers working for CFO and JTC would informally coordinate their specifications wherever interdependencies existed. Such interchange is normal practice in the United States. However, IEI was very reluctant to show any of its tentative plans to CRS Sirrine (CRSS). IEI said that because its plans were interrelated it could not discuss specifications until all of its work was completed. The implication was that IEI would carry out its assigned task as it chose. And in practice CRSS and CFO saw almost none of the detailed drawings and specifications covering equipment outside the battery limits until the Technology Transfer Contract was virtually completed. And that was too late to do much coordination.

This lack of coordination promptly enough to allow adjustments did not arise from ill-will. Rather, it came from different ways that outside engineers perceive their roles. CRSS sees itself as a part of its client's team. IEI sees itself as an independent professional body which completes assignments according to its own work schedules and standards.

Summary

In conclusion, we should stress that an excellent Technology Transfer Contract did emerge from the negotiations. Because vague points were discussed and clarified—"nailed down" in American slang—fewer difficulties turned up during plant construction. The plant is running as planned. NCFC is progressing much better than other joint ventures where difficult issues were merely postponed for later consideration.

Nevertheless, the negotiations were indeed slow and frustrating.

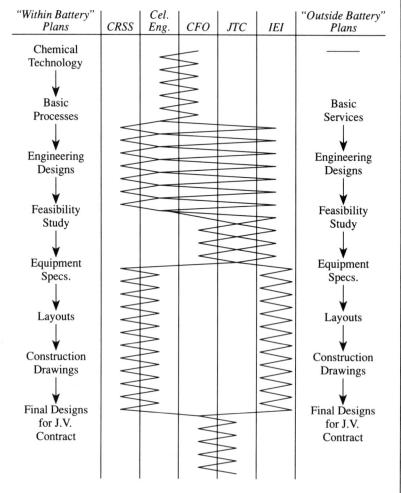

FIGURE 8-2
Schematic Diagram of
Intergroup Discussions Promoting Coordination of Plans
for Nantong Plant

CFO = Celanese Fibers Operation
JTC = Jiangsu Tobacco Company
CRSS = CRS Sirrine (U.S. engineering firm)
IEI = Industry Engineering Institute advising JTC
Cel. Eng. = Celanese Engineers assigned to NCFC

Certainly future negotiations can move along better than they did for NCFC in 1984 to 1987.

Reasons for delay. When negotiations for the NCFC joint venture started in October 1984 the Chinese officials of CNTC hoped to break ground for the new plant a year later. In practice, reaching agreement on just the transfer of the processing technology took longer than a year. Four reasons contributed to this delay.

1. The contract goes into much more detail than do many other joint venture contracts.

2. Chinese regulations then in effect forced the negotiators to try to meet standards for a Technology Purchase Contract even though many of these standards were not appropriate for a joint venture like NCFC.

3. IEI, the engineering advisor to JTC, felt obliged to follow strictly the standard guidelines for a Technology Purchase Contract, and JTC was reluctant to try to secure liberal interpretations or exceptions to these guidelines. Months were lost in repetitious questioning.

4. More broadly, the government regulations focused on protection from foreign exploitation more than on using joint ventures to secure the benefits of cooperation.

Guidelines for future negotiators. The experience of JTC and CFO in working out an agreement for transferring technology suggests several guidelines for negotiators of other joint ventures.

a. Try to shift the focus away from protection against exploitation and win-lose bargaining. Instead, seek a fair basis for continuing cooperation. More specifically, 1) look for guidelines relevant to joint ventures to replace those developed for Technology Purchase Contracts. 2) Try to minimize secret instructions—such as "little green books"—which cannot be openly confronted by the prospective partners.

b. Extend the agreement beyond generalities. Push the discussions and agreement to specific processes, equipment, volumes, and the like. This uncovers potential problems, clarifies the resulting agreement, and provides a more solid base for other planning. Such an extension will probably require that operating personnel as well as senior managers join in the discussion.

c. When planning tasks are divided among several parties, provide for frequent exchanges of tentative plans so that coordination can take place early before designs and specifications are "frozen."

d. Turn requests for output guarantees into a multi-sided commitment regarding all key inputs and outputs. In other words, recognize that the total operation must be brought up to standard if results are to be guaranteed.

Chapter 9

Preparing for Joint Venture Operations

Technology for processing raw materials, discussed in the preceding chapter, is only one facet in planning a new venture. Other resources and know-how are essential in creating an active business based on the new plant. The present chapter deals with these other resources and know-how. Resources for two stages are involved.

Project Organization and Operating Organization

Building a house differs sharply from living in it. Likewise, constructing a modern tow plant and even adding trained operators differs from actually running the tow business.

This distinction became important in drawing up the joint venture contract for NCFC (Nantong Cellulose Fibers Company). The joint venture is concerned not just with a turnkey plant; it also expects to be an operating enterprise for at least fifteen years. Inevitably, however, much of the negotiation between JTC and CFO centered on what each party would contribute (or pay for) in getting the new plant ready to run. Thinking about the later operating stage—when "they" and "us" became merged into "we"—tended to get pushed into the background.

One very helpful arrangement that was used to distinguish between and still give attention to both stages was establishing a separate "preparation and construction office," as required by joint venture regulations. This office had full responsibility for getting the plant built and executing other provisions of the joint venture contract. At the "end of the start-up" (defined in the Technology Transfer Contract) the office was to be dissolved. In other words, the construction stage was organized as a distinct project.

This preparation and construction office had a manager, plus four groups (general planning, technical, equipment/material, and financial) each headed by a deputy manager; and a maximum of 15 persons from CFO and 90 persons from JTC. Once the project was completed the organization was to be phased out and the personnel re-assigned.

On the other hand, the Joint Venture Contract also established a business management office responsible for the daily operation and management of the new company. This is the continuing organization that picks up operations as the preparation and construction office phases out. It has a general manager reporting to the Board of Directors, three deputy general managers, and so on.

Advantages of this dual organization included: 1) Responsibility for construction was clear, and work could move forward promptly without waiting for the basic structure to be established. 2) The company did not become over-staffed with construction supervisors whose skills did not fit the continuing operating organization. 3) Materials and cash flows for construction could be isolated and more easily controlled. 4) A streamlined operating organization could be more clearly planned.

Right Number of Right People

For the preparation and construction office, a temporary organization, the primary personnel questions dealt with recruiting and paying the people who administered the program. Most of the actual construction work, of course, was done by outside contractors.

The JTC and CFO negotiations set limits on the number of employees in this office—105 in total. Also, the party responsible for paying the base salaries and transportation costs to China for all CFO employees was carefully specified, as were local living costs, local travel, overseas premiums, home leave, and the like.

More attention was given to the staffing of the continuing organization. Since employment practices in China differ greatly from those in the United States, personnel administration has been a source of trouble in most Chinese/foreign ventures.

By the time the NCFC joint venture contract was negotiated the Chinese government had published a special set of regulations for employment in Chinese/foreign joint ventures. These new regulations deal with many of the labor difficulties that foreign managers had encountered in China. Consequently, the JTC and CFO negotiators were able, with a minimum of discussion, to agree on a set of "Labor Principles" and trade union relationships.

Among the "principles" that are important to Western managers are:

- Selection of workers on the basis of qualifications and skills needed by the company and demonstrated in a test period within the company.
- Management authority to dismiss surplus workers and workers who are not performing satisfactorily.
- Management authority to assign tasks to each worker according to the needs of the company.
- Starting wages in a range of 120% to 150% of wages paid for similar work in state-run enterprises in the local city (Nantong).
- Management authority to give material rewards to workers who show fine achievement in their work, and—after consultation with the employees union—to fine or dismiss a worker who violates the regulations of the company.

If these principles, which are explicitly stated in the joint venture contract, can be skillfully executed the operating organization of NCFC has an opportunity to be highly effective and efficient.

In addition, the joint venture contract sets the maximum number of employees in the company, a figure that can be changed only by the board of directors.

Another crucial chapter in the agreement called for the selection and extensive training of a group of highly competent Chinese people who would be placed in key positions in the continuing organization of NCFC. The individuals were to be carefully selected jointly by JTC and CFO for their technical capabilities and management skills, and had to be able (or learn) to communicate in both oral and written English. Then CFO (at its expense) was to provide this group with six months of training in a Celanese plant in the United States. This was a substantial commitment by CFO of the time and effort of Celanese managers in the U.S. Plant technology, quality control, maintenance, safety, and other aspects of plant operations were to be covered; the training was to be completed prior to start-up of the Nantong plant.

This special group was expected to serve as the critical core of the battery limits production group. Their experience in the United States and their command of English as well as Chinese should aid substantially in effective use of CFO know-how in China. Because of their special training each Trainee had to agree to remain an employee of NCFC for at least five years; and NCFC agreed to use its best efforts to assure that the important, long-term employment relationship would not be disturbed by anybody.

CFO further agreed to recruit up to four U.S. personnel for management and technical positions in the continuing organization.

Of course, by stipulating the employment of both U.S. and Chinese managers the troublesome issue arises of how their respective salaries should compare. The compensation needed to induce a competent and experienced U.S. manager to move to what for him is a strange and lonely assignment looks very high to his Chinese counterpart. However, if an equivalent amount in RMB is paid to a Chinese manager a sharp disparity is created in the local salary structure. What's fair in similar circumstances has troubled most foreign ventures in developing countries.

The NCFC agreement postpones a show-down on this matter. In the near term, foreign managers are to be paid a salary and other benefits equal to those paid to comparable personnel by CFO in the United States plus a foreign living allowance. Chinese managers are to be paid an amount ranging from 120% to 150% of the wage actually received by personnel in comparable positions in state-run enterprises in Nantong. In other words, the prevailing salary level in each manager's home-base is the chief guide.

However, provisions were made for the NCFC Board of Directors to review and revise the Chinese managers' salary scheme at an appropriate time, including the question of foreign/Chinese salary parity. Note that the regulations permit salary parity but it is not mandatory.

*   *   *

A concluding note regarding employment: For all of the issues the joint venture agreement makes a clear distinction between personnel for the preparation and construction office and personnel for the continuing business management office. And when dealing with the latter the long-run capability of the new company is a dominant concern.

Purchasing Sources

The new company needed things as well as employees; so the joint venture agreement has chapters dealing especially with purchasing sources.

One general guideline is clear—materials, equipment, and supplies are to be purchased from producers in the People's Republic of China if items of satisfactory quality, delivery, and price are available. Having accepted this principle, the joint venture agreement could focus on exceptions; what is to be imported from what suppliers.

For the plant construction, the amount of imported equipment was large and CFO was responsible for supplying it. Most of this equipment was for inside the battery limits and was even listed in the Equipment Investment Principles which are part of the joint venture contract. One reason for this amount of detail was to avoid the use of foreign exchange; the cost of this imported equipment became part of CFO's investment in the joint venture, and consequently did not require foreign exchange.

During the operating stage of the joint venture, in contrast, imports must be paid for in hard currency. This places such imports under closer scrutiny. The importation of two sorts of products, both crucial to the maintenance of the quality of tow produced, is anticipated in the agreement. One is cellulose acetate flake, the major raw material for the plant (currently unavailable in China), and the other is special replacement parts.

A separate flake supply agreement was included in the overall joint venture agreement. In effect, it stipulates the manner in which NCFC shall obtain its flake until specification grade flake becomes available from a producer within China.

This flake agreement is an example of synergies that should be sought in a joint venture. The flake is to be purchased at the prevailing international price, and must meet the flake specifications set forth in the CFO technology package.

Although not part of the Nantong plant agreement, there is a less formal understanding between CNTC and CFO with respect to finished tow that CNTC imports. CFO is a preferred, *not exclusive,* foreign source of tow—again at international terms and prices. As we noted in Part I, the Chinese used their foreign purchases as an attraction to foreign companies who will help build China's domestic production capacity.

Note that again a clear separation of provision for NCFC's construction stage and its operating stage was made. And the arrangement for purchasing flake during the operating stage was satisfactory to CFO and did put NCFC in a sound long-run supply position.

Production Know-How

Like the personnel and material supply provisions, the production chapters in the joint venture agreement deal with continuing operations as well as with the construction stage.

The Technology Transfer Contract, as we explained in the preceding chapter, is part of the overall agreement and it focuses mainly on getting the new plant constructed and into operation. Nevertheless, several provisions go further.

1. During the period of the agreement (15 years), provision is made for the procedure of keeping NCFC's manufacturing technology current. Thus, NCFC will continue to have access to state-of-the-art technology throughout this period; it need not spend a lot of its funds on research in order to keep up with world advances.

2. Details of the processing technology, however, are secret. Production people, IEI personnel and others who have participated in specific production planning—or will do so—are all prohibited from describing the process to outsiders. In other words, CFO's technology is not to become public knowledge.

3. The licenses to use CFO's technology apply only to the Nantong site. Also, products made at the Nantong plant may not be sold outside of the People's Republic of China without the unanimous consent of the Board of Directors. This means that in the foreseeable future NCFC will be a domestic supplier and not enter into the global market.

Briefly, at least in terms of production technology, the joint venture agreement assures that the new Nantong plant will be among the best in the world. The agreement goes further. It provides a way for NCFC to have access to advances in technology so that the Nantong plant can maintain its high position for the next fifteen years—without necessarily spending its own funds on research and development.

However, as now planned this capability is to be confined to the Nantong plant, and the Nantong plant is to concentrate on serving the needs for tow within the P.R.C. In fact, the size of the domestic market far exceeds the present and projected capacity of the Nantong plant; so these constraints are no hardship on the joint venture.

Marketing and Accounting

Centralized marketing of NCFC output is clearly implied in the joint venture agreement. CNTC will perform most of the marketing for NCFC because of its role in China's tobacco industry.

More specifically, as administrator of the tobacco monopoly, CNTC has power to regulate the production of filter cigarettes by each local cigarette plant. This, in turn, determines the demand for tow by each plant. In addition, because of the scarcity of foreign exchange with which to buy imported tow, the domestic output of NCFC will be preferred and will have to be allocated by CNTC. Such allocation by CNTC will, of course, simplify NCFC's marketing task.

Likewise, the constraint on export sales—just noted above—simplifies marketing. NCFC's marketing in the foreseeable future will consist primarily of physical distribution, and it is possible that a centralized unit within CNTC will undertake this function.

Modern accounting, like marketing, receives limited attention in the joint venture agreement. This explicit provision says that international accounting practices will be used—except as required otherwise by Chinese law. This applies to accounting records used for internal control, for calculation of profit and distribution to various funds, and for reporting to outside organizations. While not specifically stated in the agreement, international accounting practice does require separation of construction outlays from operating income and expense. Thus, the way is open for a clear set of financial controls over operations.

Conclusions

The joint venture agreement—pages long—contains much detail about personnel, purchasing, production, marketing, and accounting that we have only summarized here. Nevertheless, two dominant themes emerge.

1. The preparation and construction of the plant has been recognized as a separate undertaking with its own organization, guidelines, resources, and completion targets. This has been treated as a major project that ends with the plant start-up, at which time its temporary organization is to be disbanded.

Meanwhile, an organization for the operation of the company after the plant has been started is to be developed. A continuing management structure, carefully trained managers, material supply, and other features needed for long-run operations are to be put in place. Although some individuals may move from jobs in the construction projects to jobs in the operating organization, the distinction has been maintained throughout the contract negotiations. And that distinction between building the plant and then running it has aided both planning and control.

2. Even more impressive is the nature of the joint venture operations that emerge. NCFC will be a classic example of what management experts now call a "focused factory." A focused factory is designed a) to serve a particular market need b) with the best available resources and technology for the operations it is to perform, and c) minimum outlays for other activities that can be more efficiently done by outside organizations.

Consistent with this focused factory concept, provisions have been made for marketing, research and development, and foreign supply of materials. This leaves NCFC free to concentrate on being the most efficient and effective manufacturer in the world of cigarette tow tailored to the specific needs of the Chinese market. Significantly, all the long-run operating provisions in the joint venture contract support this particular mission for NCFC. The company's simplicity and focus can be its unique strengths.

The financing and top management structure for this tailor-made enterprise are described in the next chapters.

Chapter 10

Discipline Imposed by Financing Requirements

NCFC's construction and operating plans, summarized in the preceding chapters, needed money for their execution. Arrangements for this investment included safeguards and provision for repayment which serve as constraints on company activities. This source of internal discipline has been inserted at three control points in NCFC's life: registered capital used for construction, distribution of net income earned from operations, and provision for the termination of the joint venture.

Registered Capital

An important and intriguing feature of the financial planning was an early agreement on the amount of "registered capital" that JTC and CFO would each invest, and then the various steps taken to stay within this commitment.

During the discussions in the spring of 1985, as soon as the size of the Nantong plant was sketched out and scope of operations inside and outside the battery limits were identified, CFO and JTC each estimated the investment that would be required for their respective spheres. Although the basic concept gave CFO responsibility for facilities inside the battery limits and JTC responsibility for facilities outside the battery limits, the U.S. dollar and the Chinese RMB needs did not neatly match such separate parts of the plant. Some RMB's were needed for civil construction and assembly work within the battery limits, and some dollars were needed for special equipment and supplies outside the battery limits. With these adjustments, lists of equipment and work to be obtained by CFO with dollars, and lists of equipment and work to be obtained by JTC with RMB's, were developed.

The basic financing plan for the new venture was that CFO would supply the dollars and JTC the RMB. And by converting RMB's into dollars the relative shares of invested capital would be determined. However, capitalizing the joint venture had other considerations.

1. The total investment had to be approved by the State Planning Commission and the Commission had a strong policy of keeping total investment in joint ventures low. During 1985 a Celanese competitor was preparing its feasibility study for a Nontong plant that showed a relatively low capital investment. The JTC/CFO plan had to stay close to this figure.

2. Also, the relative positions of JTC and CFO had status and policy implications for both of the negotiating parties. Fortunately CFO wanted to be a minority partner, and JTC needed to be a majority partner.

Recognizing these and related considerations, the negotiators agreed that the "registered capital" should be:

JTC	$18,300,000	69.32%
CFO	$ 8,100,000	30.68%
Total	$26,400,000	100.00%

Moreover, the agreement included lists of equipment, supplies, and work (RMB items) that JTC was to provide, and lists of equipment and supplies (dollar items) that CFO was to provide.

An important feature was that the registered capital figures were to remain fixed even though the actual outlays for the listed inputs turned out to be more, or less, than the amounts stated in the table.

At the time the registered capital figures were agreed upon, CFO expected that its inputs would cost more than $8,100,000. On the other hand, JTC anticipated that its inputs might cost less than $18,300,000. Indeed, the joint venture contract provides that JTC's equity share of the company capital shall not be changed even if the actual value of its contribution is less than $18,300,000.

By the end of 1987 it became clear that the costs of JTC's inputs had been underestimated and would exceed the $18,300,000. CFO outlays also exceeded their stated value. However, the registered capital figures had been used in the approved joint venture contract; to make a change would reopen the Chinese government approval process. So, plans for capital sources were not renegotiated.

Another example of sticking to agreed limits was anticipated in the final joint venture agreement. The cost of sundry equipment and supplies for outside-the-battery limits to be purchased with CFO's dollars was difficult to estimate. So a part of the registered capital agreement was that CFO would make a specified U.S. dollar amount available for this purpose. Stainless steel pipes, automobiles, fork-lift trucks, typewriters, and an array of other items were involved. As might be expected, the number of such imported items which became attractive grew, and soon CFO was asked to spend beyond the stipulated limit. Here again, CFO held the line. CFO was willing to change the list; but if, say, a microcomputer was to be added something else had to be deleted to hold the total within the limit.

At least two guidelines are suggested by this experience with registered capital.

1. For key figures on the capital contributions of each partner, detailed planning is aided by settling on informal and reasonable amounts—and then holding to that agreement. The agreed-upon figures may be estimates which deviate from reality by the time the planning is completed—as was the case in writing the NCFC joint venture agreement. Nevertheless, starting assumptions are needed around which other agreements are made. Without such planning premises, the entire planning and negotiating process is in flux; no one knows what to count on. If the premises are unexpectedly changed, a lot of related plans should be reexamined.

2. Holding the line rarely will be easy. Pressures of the moment seem compelling. This is especially true in international relationships

because the parties see benefits to themselves and sacrifices of others quite differently. In the NCFC case the planning achieved an integrity and consistency because key premises were maintained. Even the process of planning became a different kind of management technique. It changed from "What equipment would we like to have?" to "What is the best use of a fixed total sum that will be available?" Choices had to be made.

Distribution of Net Income

Plans for distributing net income, of course, shift the focus from NCFC's start-up to its long-run operations. The joint venture agreement anticipates that when the company becomes profitable quite diverse pressures will arise concerning the use of that net income. Understandably, in a developing country any flow of net income will be coveted.

The negotiators tried to set some guidelines which would keep the new company healthy while meeting the reasonable expectations of the founding parties.

One move sought to avoid having net income taxed away. Recent Chinese legislation is designed to block inequitable levies by local governments, and JTC was assigned the task of helping NCFC obtain as favorable tax treatment as the laws allow.

Another provision sets limits on the contributions that NCFC will make to three special funds that are recognized in Chinese business practice. More specifically, the annual contribution limits are:

	Maximum percentage of annual after-tax profit
Reserve fund	5%
Expansion fund	5%
Bonus and welfare fund:	5%, or $100,000, whichever is larger

After the allocations for these three funds, then the remaining net profit is to be distributed to JTC and CFO in proportion to their shares of registered capital.

Note that the presumption is that all profits will be distributed each year—to the funds and to the capital investors. Plowing back profits in expansion, so common in U.S. corporations, is not part of the NCFC plan. (Cash needed for inventory, accounts receivable, and other short-run purposes is to be borrowed.)

These provisions for distribution of profits may seem premature for a company that was not yet in existence and had to build a new plant from the ground up. Nevertheless, they did clarify to various interested organizations what the distribution pattern was expected to be. And by including the profit distribution plan in the joint venture agreement that plan was endorsed by the central government reviewing organizations along with all the other arrangements.

Provision for Termination of the Company

When the joint venture agreement expires after fifteen years, the joint venture per se is to be terminated. The plan is for CFO to receive a specific compensation for its equity. Then all the remaining assets go to JTC.

To assure that NCFC has funds available to make this final compensation to CFO, NCFC will accumulate the required funds over the term of the joint venture. In effect, this accumulation is like the U.S. practice of a "sinking fund" used to retire bonds.

The relation of accumulated termination funds to "net income" and to cash flow pose differences in what Chinese and Westerners mean by "net income." The Chinese usually think of net income (or profit) as a cash gain. Under that view the funds are a reduction in profits available for other uses. Under Western ("international") accounting practice the accumulated funds continue to be an asset and therefore is not an expense which would reduce the net income. At the same time, however, Westerners make a non-cash charge against income for depreciation of fixed assets. Since the annual depreciation on NCFC's plant will probably exceed the required funds, the differences in viewpoints on "net income" probably will not pose a practical problem. If NCFC is at least breaking even on the Western profit and loss statement, it should be able to accumulate the required funds.

Nevertheless, the long-run implications of the termination plan are large from a strictly financial viewpoint. Some might consider CFO as only an investor, not a part owner. In addition to a share in whatever net income may be earned, it is to receive the termination compensation at the end of fifteen years. Indeed, if the joint venture agreement is ended in less than fifteen years CFO is to receive such compensation from the company or by JTC at that time. CFO does not own any assets located in China, nor does it have any continuing claim on the earnings of the Nantong plant after the joint venture is terminated.

In contrast, JTC gets the plant, other assets, and the on-going business when the joint venture is ended. Insofar as ownership and "equity" have meaning in communist China, they will belong to JTC.

So, looking at just the present joint venture in just the dimensions shown on the accounting statements, CFO may want to maximize net earnings during the 15-year period, and may be indifferent to results thereafter. JTC will have a longer horizon and might be willing to sacrifice short-term earnings for future benefits.

This difference in pertinent time-spans for CFO and for JTC is reflected in the requirements for unanimous decisions by NCFC's board of directors—to be described in the next chapter. Even more significant is the inadequacy of accounting statements to show all the dimensions of the joint venture—a point to be emphasized in the final chapter of Part II.

Conclusions Relating to Financing

Americans typically think that a "joint venture" includes a sharing by the partners in the ownership of the new enterprise. And with respect to NCFC the allocations to JTC and CFO of registered capital and membership on the board of directors tend to support this viewpoint. Such a concept of shared ownership, however, does *not* fit NCFC because of the terms of the termination agreement.

CFO is making an investment in NCFC for only a period of 15 years, at which time the termination compensation is to be paid to CFO in hard dollars. In financial terms, CFO's investment could be considered an interest free *long-term loan*—not a share in the equity (ownership) of the enterprise.

CFO was willing to enter into this joint venture and make this long-term loan because of the potential benefits that are associated with it. These benefits include, during the 15-year term, a) 30.68% of NCFC's net income after payments into the three funds, and b) sales of tow to CNTC and acetate flake to NCFC—at international prices. Also important is a working relationship with CNTC and its affiliates that may lead to other investments and/or sales.

Recognizing the limited time and the uncertainties surrounding the benefits from making the loan, CFO does have several protections: 1) Explicit provisions are made for obtaining dollars to pay CFO its share of net income and to pay CFO its termination compensation. 2) Clear limits on CFO's total investment exist. 3) CFO shares in the management of NCFC, and has equal representation with JTC on NCFC's board of directors—as explained in the next chapter.

Note that this confining of CFO's investment to a protected term loan is compatible with the focused factory concept discussed in the preceding chapter. NCFC is a clearly defined project which is limited in scope and in time. It can stand alone by itself, with benefits and restraints for each of the founding parties. The joint venture is structured so that it can be fully dissolved at the end of fifteen years, with each founder having benefited from the relationship.

Nevertheless, each party expects that their relationship will be expanded and extended beyond this first NCFC project. Indeed, the joint venture contract includes a brief statement that enlarging the plant and building a separate plant to produce acetate flake will be considered after NCFC becomes a registered company.

The economic and financial soundness of the NCFC venture is not dependent upon such expansion. A highlight of the way this cigarette tow plan is put together is that the first Nantong technology/market agreement is sound and self-sufficient by itself—while at the same time it opens the way for other mutually attractive ventures.

Guidelines for the future. The financing aspects of the NCFC joint venture suggest several guidelines for other future Chinese/foreign enterprises.

1. Because of differences between PRC and the West in their concepts of ownership, and economic uncertainties over long periods, narrowing cooperative enterprises to self-liquidating projects of relatively short duration is attractive for the 1990s.

2. These focused projects, however, should be designed to open the way for future cooperative ventures. A succession of mutually attractive joint venture projects will typically be preferable to a far-ranging contract, at least in the currently dynamic situation. The flexibility and adaptability of a succession of agreements offsets the uncertainty inherent in the step-by-step approach.

3. Financing of each shorter-range, focused venture can and should be "tight." The amounts of investment should be limited to what is

justified by the particular project. Also, explicit provisions should be included for an adequate return on the investment—through a share of the net income, return of the principal, or other cash flows; and, foreign exchange sources for these payments should be specified.

This way of financing each venture inserts a discipline on the use of scarce resources. It avoids the assumption that high profits elsewhere will in some unknown way justify lax controls on current activities.

4. While careful financing of each joint venture is crucial, it is only one dimension of a well planned cooperative enterprise. Other important aspects such as technology transfers, market position, public support, and global competition do not show up immediately on financial reports. So, the challenge is to fit sound financing into wise arrangements for these other dimensions.

Chapter 11

Top Management Structure

The many plans for NCFC, briefly summarized in the preceding chapters, lay out a course for constructing the new plant and developing a distinctive "focused factory" enterprise. To convert these plans into reality a "make-happen" top management structure was needed. So, provisions for senior management positions and a board of directors were included in the joint venture contract.

Organization Design

Responsibility for getting the new plant built and into operation was centered on a manager of the preparation and construction office, and four deputy managers. Continuing operations were placed under a general manager of the company and three deputy general managers, with department managers reporting to this group. This general structure, sketched in Exhibit 11-1, had the advantages of being simple and customary.

More debate came in deciding whether these positions would be filled by Chinese or Westerners. Getting a plant built and running in

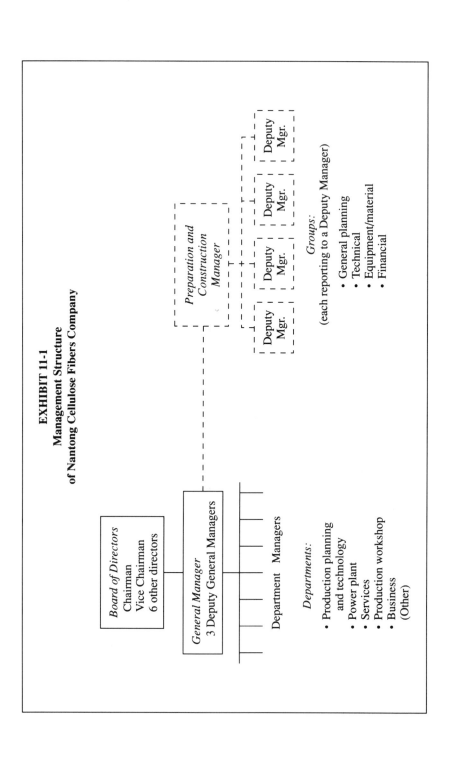

EXHIBIT 11-1
Management Structure
of Nantong Cellulose Fibers Company

Board of Directors
Chairman
Vice Chairman
6 other directors

General Manager
3 Deputy General Managers

Department Managers

Departments:

- Production planning and technology
- Power plant
- Services
- Production workshop
- Business
- (Other)

Preparation and Construction Manager

Deputy Mgr.   Deputy Mgr.   Deputy Mgr.   Deputy Mgr.

Groups:
(each reporting to a Deputy Manager)

- General planning
- Technical
- Equipment/material
- Financial

Nantong involved negotiations with diverse Chinese organizations, so the head of the preparation and construction office was to be Chinese. His four deputies were to be two Chinese and two Americans; in addition, CFO agreed to provide technical experts as needed for shorter assignments. The dominant factor in making these selections was the kinds of skills most needed to get the plant up and running.

The management structure laid out for continuing operations was also straightforward, having functional department managers reporting to the General Manager and his three Deputy General Managers. The "focused factory" concept puts emphasis on production and has little need for complex organization. A single location should help communication among the management team.

The first General Manager for four years is to be a Westerner selected by CFO; thereafter, appointments to this position will rotate every three years by selections first from CFO and then from JTC. For Deputy General Managers, JTC is to appoint two and CFO one. Although not stipulated in the joint venture contract, the expectation was that department manager positions would be filled from the sixteen Chinese who would receive six months of training by CFO in the United States.

Under these plans the number of CFO personnel stationed in China will decrease as time passes. The preparation and construction office will disappear entirely, and the General Manager's office will have a maximum of four Americans. With the sixteen trainees back from the United States, the expectation is that shortly after the plant startup is completed, transferable parts of U.S. management practice will have been absorbed and the expense of expatriate managers can be reduced.

A Balanced Board of Directors

The NCFC board of directors has two broad functions. 1) Through advice and decisions it is responsible for the effective and efficient operations of the company. Also, 2) its members represent the interests of the two founding parties—JTC and CFO. Inevitably, the interests of the company itself, of JTC, and of CFO will not always be the same. The board of directors, then, is the body where differences in objectives are reconciled and different proposals for company action are mediated.

In theory, at least, all of the persons in managerial positions are committed to making the company itself strong and efficient, regardless of who selected them. They are not placed within the management structure to be an advocate of a "stakeholder" (founding party, union, local government, customers, and the like). Instead, the board of directors is the place where diverse interests are weighed and merged into a consistent program for the company.

During the early (1984) discussions of a possible joint venture it was stated that this would be a 50/50 partnership with each party having an equal representation on the board of directors. Because of this agreement CFO and JTC were willing to approach the design of the management structure in terms of what would best serve the new company.

Later, when the joint venture agreement was being put in final form, the following statement in the government regulations for joint ventures was raised:

> ". . . the distribution of members of the board is to be determined by discussion of the two major parties with reference to the ratio of capital contributions."

The Chinese negotiators said that in view of the division of registered capital and the latter part of the above regulation, CFO should appoint three directors and JTC seven. Stultz, who had read the regulations carefully, pointed out that the two parties were obliged only to give attention to the registered capital ratio in their discussion—and that this had been done earlier when four JTC and four CFO directors had been agreed upon.

The issue here was whether the joint venture should be treated merely as financial investment or as a long-run cooperative relationship. As we have already seen, the registered capital figures were not exact and both JTC and CFO had interests and made contributions far beyond the registered capital. So the broader view of the joint venture was taken, and the previous agreement on four directors each for JTC and CFO was honored.

Unanimous Decision by the Board of Directors

Agreement on who would select directors did not fully resolve issues surrounding the board. Questions arose about officers of the board of directors and about protection of the sponsoring organizations on crucial decisions.

For foreign joint ventures in China generally, one sponsor names the chairman of the board and the other sponsor names the vice chairman. However, for NCFC, CFO agreed that JTC would designate both the chairman and the vice chairman from its four directors. This arrangement enables JTC to give a prestigious title to a person in Nanjing— the capital city in Jiangsu Province and also to a person in Nantong where the plant is located. Good external relationships in both cities are important.

Protection for the two sponsoring organizations is more subtle. While CNTC on the Chinese side and Hoechst Celanese, USA on the American side are quite willing to have the NCFC board decide most matters by majority vote, they want more control over crucial decisions such as a merger, diversifying into a new business, sale of assets, and the like. The difficulty of attending board meetings halfway around the world adds to the risk of unwelcome slip-ups.

This problem is more serious for the Americans than for the Chinese. The Chinese have a well developed custom of consulting key officials and each other before taking a position on important matters. And after a position is established they are well disciplined to vote as a unified block.

In contrast, the Americans are more individualistic. They want each person to express his opinion so that a full range of facts and viewpoints can be considered in reaching a final decision. For example, they would want an American General Manager to be a member of the board of directors, and would expect the General Manager to state which course of action he thought was wise even when that course differed from the choice of some other American director. A split vote among American directors is quite possible. This exposes the sponsoring organization if decisions can be made by a majority vote of the directors.

So, to protect key sponsors on crucial decisions a level of unanimous agreement by all directors was specified in the joint venture contract. The issues on which full endorsement is required are summarized in Exhibit 11-2.

Note that the unanimous decision list includes issues which are important to keeping NCFC in a "focused factory" role (described in Chapter 9). Also included are possible changes that might undermine NCFC's ability to meet the financial controls described in Chapter 10. The need for a unanimous decision likewise assures that any deviations from the basic mission of the joint venture will receive a careful review by the entire board of directors.

This arrangement for unanimous decision on key issues does reduce

---

EXHIBIT 11-2
Summary of Decisions
Requiring Unanimous Agreement by Board of Directors

Company existence and assets

Termination; extension of joint venture period
Merger with, or investment in, third party
Transfer or lease of major assets

Financing

Increase in registered capital
Changes in allocation of net income

Personnel matters

Appointment and pay of General Managers, Deputy General Managers,
    and other top-ranking employees
Total number of company employees
Significant labor programs

Scope of business

New products and new businesses
Sales outside of PRC

Operating plans and results

Schedules and budgets of preparation and construction office
Annual plans for tow production
Approval of annual balance sheets and profit and loss statements

---

the need for controls by JTC and CFO at other places in the organization. CFO is less concerned about putting its own sentries in operating positions. NCFC has more flexibility to run day-to-day activities in a way that fits its own local needs.

On the other hand, this tight rein at the board level will, of course, make changes in NCFC strategy difficult. But such an arrangement is consistent with the plan to repay CFO and dissolve the joint venture in fifteen years. The aim is a single, well defined thrust, not a center for innovation and diversification.

We should note that expansion and change are not ruled out entirely. The joint venture agreement does say:

After this contract is approved and the Company is registered, the Board of Directors of the Company shall determine the desirability of

a. expanding the capacity of the Plant . . .
b. increasing the varieties of tow produced at the Plant
c. including in the project the production of cellulose acetate flake, a raw material used by the Plant.

However, such changes would call for a lot of modifications in the present well integrated joint venture contract. A new set of mutual understandings would be necessary. Meanwhile the present agreement has a clear narrow focus.

Moreover, if the present joint venture lives up to expectations, Celanese and/or CNTC may have other opportunities for constructive joint ventures. Flexibility at the strategy level is likely to be found in a series of sharply focused ventures rather than blurring the neatness and efficiency of NCFC. Probably NCFC's board of directors can contribute most to such an array of joint ventures by making NCFC an outstanding success in its selected niche.

Conclusion

The NCFC top management structure is well suited to focus on making this Chinese/foreign joint venture an outstanding success. The structure is simple and not overloaded with unneeded personnel. The provision for unanimous decisions by the board of directors on key issues will discourage changes in NCFC's mission.

By centering attention on reliable and efficient operations, this top management can demonstrate how a well conceived, focused joint venture should operate. Indeed, an opportunity exists for becoming a model for other single-mission joint ventures.

Initiative for expanding the scope of cooperation between CNTC and Celanese is expected to come directly from these organizations, leaving NCFC free to concentrate on its clearly defined operating role.

Guidelines for the future. PRC needs examples of how it can run large state-of-the-art plants efficiently. NCFC is one approach. A simple top management structure coupled with a clearly defined mission provides an opportunity to concentrate on excellence in operations.

Other joint ventures might well seek structures which provide similar simple, uncluttered operating units—where top management can focus on being the best performer in its industry.

Chapter 12

Securing Central Government Approval

Even agreement between JTC and CFO on the quite specific features of their joint venture, reviewed in the preceding chapters, left the launching process incomplete. Approval of the plan by the appropriate central government agencies was also necessary. Indeed, many proposed Chinese/foreign joint ventures bog down in this approval process.

This chapter reviews several steps that the creators of the Nantong venture took to successfully clear the approval hurdle. Just writing down various aspects of the agreement in clear, enforceable language was a substantial task; merging U.S. and Chinese law relating to joint ventures was involved. And as often happens when thoughts are put into writing, new needs emerge for refinements and additions to the understanding. Time slipped by, as we shall note, until the pressure to get into action curtailed discussion. The go-ahead signal finally was given two and a half years after CNTC and Celanese recognized that they had an attractive basis for a joint venture.

Time Required for Central Approval

Approval of a joint venture the size of NCFC is a multi-stage process. In addition to numerous informal conversations, the major hurdles in the present case were:

1. Acceptance of the basic plan to produce cigarette tow in one or more domestic plants—using foreign technology.

2. Approval by the State Planning Commission of a joint feasibility study for the Nantong location. As already noted, this study included plans for a technology transfer to the proposed joint venture.

3. Approval of the specific joint venture contract by the Ministry of Foreign Economic Relations and Trade (MOFERT).

In other ventures comparable to NCFC any one of these hurdles might require several lengthy revisions or refinements of an original proposal. For example, a proposed joint venture contract with a major U.S. based company for cigarette production took over two years and several reiterations before it was approved by MOFERT.

In contrast, the JTC/CFO proposals were worked out with care and in quite specific terms. Also, early in the negotiating process LEC had arranged informal meetings of Celanese managers with government officials so that the approvers were dealing with known ideas and known people. Partly as a result of this preparatory work, the joint feasibility study supporting the NCFC proposal was approved by the State Planning Commission (and, in effect, associated agencies) within several months of its submission; and the proposed joint venture contract was approved by MOFERT in six weeks. The chronological relation of these approval periods to the total planning process for NCFC is shown in Exhibit 12-1. Also noteworthy was the acceptance of the proposals as submitted with only very minor adjustments.

We should note that the broad plan for the tobacco industry included domestic production of cigarette tow. This was already accepted prior to Celanese involvement. And CNTC had obtained endorsement of three possible plant sites, including Nantong. So, the central approvals needed for the NCFC venture involved only a joint feasibility study and a joint venture contract with its related documents. Of course, a variety of permissions, certifications, and other agreements had to be obtained at the provincial and local levels.

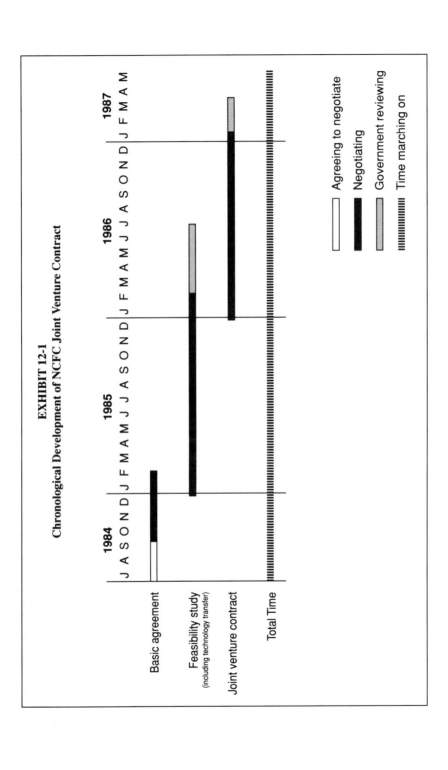

EXHIBIT 12-1
Chronological Development of NCFC Joint Venture Contract

A normal question, especially for persons wishing to promote a future joint venture in China, is what explains the relatively prompt and smooth approval experience in the NCFC case.

Overcoming the Rigidity of Technological Transfer

Transfer of technology for making acetate cigarette tow is a central feature of the NCFC joint venture. So, one might assume that the joint feasibility study and the joint venture contract would adequately cover this transfer issue. However, the People's Republic of China has a separate set of standards for technology transfer contracts—based on the assumption that only a sale of technology is being made. Inevitably some reviewing officials in the State Planning Commission or in MOFERT would expect these standards to be met even though they did not neatly fit a joint venture situation.

Consequently, the negotiations of plans for NCFC had to give careful attention to how their proposals could be reconciled with the generalized standards for a technology transfer contract. Examples of potentially troublesome issues relating to technology transfer that were resolved in the joint venture documents involved the following.

Performance guarantees. Many foreign companies are reluctant to expressly guarantee the performance of their technology in a Chinese plant because they lack control over so many of the operating conditions and materials supplies. Nevertheless, CFO did guarantee for a test period, in effect, the rate of output, product quality, and raw material usage of the equipment and processes within the battery limits of the new plant.

The other side of this agreement is that the plant has been constructed according to CFO's designs, the start-up and maintenance conform to CFO's instructions, plant personnel has been adequately trained, and raw materials and utilities coming from outside the battery limits meet design specifications. Thus, there are guaranties on both sides of the technology transfer.

Note that this sort of mutual obligation to make the plant work as designed is aided by its setting within a joint venture. The technology transfer is not a trade at a Mid-Eastern bazaar; rather, both parties have a strong and continuing interest in having the plant work as planned.

Royalties dependent on exports. A somewhat optimistic feature of the standard Chinese concept for technological transfers is that part of the products resulting from the transfer will be exported, and the foreign exchange generated by these exports must be sufficient to cover royalties and other commitments due to the company providing the technology.

NCFC clearly does not expect to meet this standard; all the tow output will be used in China! However, all (not just part) of the output will replace current imports. Such "import substitution" will improve China's net foreign exchange balance as surely, and more simply, than exports.

In 1984 when discussions of the NCFC joint venture started, exports appealed to Chinese planners much more than import substitution. Nevertheless, the review of the feasibility study helped to clarify the benefits of replacing imports. With this recognition the export standard for technology transfers, in effect, was met.

Restrictions on use of technology. If carried to the extreme, communist doctrine would dictate that knowledge—including technology know-how—is a public asset. In contrast, most Western countries recognize patents and other proprietary knowledge, and assume that companies may place some restrictions on the use of technology which they transfer.

In this difficult area a practical compromise was made. JTC wanted to place a time-limit (15 years) on the life of the joint venture. Also, JTC wanted access to any improvements in technology that CFO might commercialize during this 15-year period. On the other side, CFO wished to confine the use of its technology to the Nantong plant where CFO was a party to the joint venture. And CFO wanted to keep tow produced in the Nantong plant out of an already crowded world market, at least for the term of the joint venture. So, all these provisions were included in the proposal presented in the joint feasibility study.

As these examples of guarantees, import substitution, and scope of the use of the technology illustrate—the NCFC feasibility study focused on a quite specific proposal. The proposed technology transfer contract was not just a general standardized form. Instead, the transfer contract included modifications which made it a practical plan for a joint venture and both JTC and CFO would actively support.

Consequently, when the State Planning Commission was assessing the joint feasibility study for NCFC it was at the same time considering refinements in the technology transfer contract that fitted the specific joint venture.

At this stage in the negotiations, then, the detailed and time-consuming work on technology transfer began to pay off. The technology transfer parts of the feasibility study that the State Planning Commission reviewed were not just a set of estimates; they were a carefully negotiated plan of action. Moreover, the more comprehensive and concrete approval that the State Planning Commission was able to give this sort of a feasibility study speeded up MOFERT's approval of the final joint venture contract.

Preparing the Way for Approval of the Joint Feasibility Study

Plans for NCFC had to be reconciled with several guidelines for joint ventures, in addition to fitting into technological transfer concepts as just discussed. This reconciliation was done before, not after, the feasibility study was submitted for approval. The following provisions were important in this respect.

Fixed contributions of registered capital. The actual investments of capital in a project like NCFC, of course, do vary from early estimates. This raises a question about the accuracy of the investment figures contained in a feasibility study. In other joint ventures both the total actual investment and the proportions between the founding partners have differed sharply from the estimates—thereby creating a need to reconsider approval of the feasibility study.

JTC and CFO avoided this possible delay by agreeing to stick to fixed amounts of "registered capital" for each party even though their actual investments might be higher or lower. The feasibility study presented firm figures.

Moreover, the ratios of "registered capital" held by JTC and by CFO were fixed—69.32% and 30.68%, respectively. This proportion was within a range that reviewing authorities had indicated would be acceptable for joint ventures.

Sharing the voting power. Although the general regulations for joint ventures say that the proportions of "registered capital" should be considered in setting the voting power within a joint venture's board of directors, such an arrangement is not mandatory.

As explained in Chapter 10, in the first discussions between CNTC and Celanese, July 1984, the potential joint venture was explicitly described as a jointly 50/50-managed organization. This concept of mutual agreement on major moves was assumed in designing NCFC. The feasibility study incorporated this concept, and no objections by the reviewing parties were anticipated.

A competitive bid. A general PRC guideline when making contracts with foreign companies is that competing bids should be secured. CNTC did discuss joint ventures with the major world tow producers in Japan, Germany, and the United States prior to the more detailed NCFC negotiations with Celanese. And, possible tow ventures with two of these other foreign companies at Jilin or Xian are still under consideration. Thus, CNTC has been actively exploring alternative ways to develop local production of tow.

Moreover, an alternative feasibility study for the Nantong plant was given to CNTC and other Chinese regulatory bodies about the same time that the CFO/JTC feasibility study was submitted. Although this second study lacked a Chinese partner it did provide the central reviewing bodies with a competitive check on the CFO/JTC proposal.

So, the general requirement for competing bids was met. In this respect, also, the stage was set for a clear response to the NCFC proposal.

Partners were ready to act. A distinctive feature of the CFO/JTC feasibility study was the advanced stage of the planning for the proposed joint venture. The study had been prepared jointly by the two sponsoring organizations. It was quite specific about what would be done. There was mutual understanding about these terms. Each party had examined the practicality of fulfilling its assigned role. Mutual respect and trust had already developed.

In other words, this feasibility study was not just a statement of what appeared to be possible. Instead, it was a plan that the sponsoring parties were ready to carry out.

Approval of the Carefully Prepared Feasibility Study

The joint feasibility study was submitted to the State Planning Commission in mid-January 1986. But it was not approved until July of that year. In view of the carefully prepared plans, the numerous advanced discussions at the national and local levels, and the endorsement of the national monopoly directly involved, why did the go-ahead approval take a full half-year?

A new economic activity such as the production of tow by NCFC affects and/or needs the cooperation of a variety of ministries and other government bodies. Especially when resources are very scarce relative to diverse demands, each of these government bodies wants to assess the proposal from its own perspective. Important among the bodies concerned were:

Ministry of Chemical Industry and NORINCO which administer likely joint venture partners at Jilin and Xian.

Ministry of Light Industry which had administered cigarette production prior to its transfer to CNTC in 1982.

Ministry of Foreign Economic Relations and Trade which administers foreign joint venture contracts, and is concerned with import substitution.

State Administration of Foreign Exchange Control and the Bank of China which are concerned with foreign exchange for tow and acetate flake purchases, and for reimbursable expenses, payment of CFO share of profits, and provision for return of capital investment.

More generally, the National Tax Bureau of the State Council.

It took time for ministries and bureaus such as these to evaluate the NCFC proposal. A comparison with the alternative feasibility study was also involved. By July, however, the NCFC feasibility study was approved with no major modifications!

Writing an Acceptable Joint Venture Contract

The approved feasibility study, with its quite specific provisions on most issues, settled the design for the NCFC joint venture. Putting these ideas into acceptable language for the final joint venture contract was the next hurdle. (In fact, to save time and maintain momentum JTC and CFO started the writing of the joint venture contract before approval of the feasibility study was received.)

For this task both parties called in lawyers. CFO relied mainly on Celanese "in-house" lawyers who had wide experience in international legal affairs, including the granting and administration of licenses to use Celanese technology. JTC obtained the help of a lawyer from the Great Wall Economic Law Office, who had previously worked in the Foreign Investment Administration Bureau of MOFERT where he became acquainted with the procedures and people who would be involved in MOFERT's review and approval of the joint venture contract.

While writing the actual contract these lawyers performed several important tasks. 1) They made sure that the contract conformed to Chinese law—insofar as Chinese law had been established on such matters. 2) They added several provisions that are customary in international agreements of this sort. And 3) they tried to assure that the language in both the Chinese and the English versions of the contract meant the same thing, and expressed the intent of JTC and CFO.

Conforming with Chinese law. Chinese law dealing with foreign joint ventures is both new and incomplete. And several features of the NCFC contract had no legal precedent. Consequently, the Chinese lawyer had to have frequent conversations with people in MOFERT to clarify what could be done—and how to say it. Then, to cover the gaps the contract states that "international practices shall be applied in situations which are not covered by Chinese law."

Added provisions. The basic plans for the joint venture were covered in the feasibility study, and these were placed—almost verbatim—into the final joint venture contract. Several other aspects, based on international experience, were added with little debate and no significant disagreement. For example, chapters were added to the contract dealing with termination and clearance; the amendment, alteration, and discharge of the contract; liabilities for breach of contract; force majeure; and settlement of disputes.

Conforming the Chinese and English versions of the contract. To avoid misunderstandings of Chinese by CFO personnel and misunderstandings of English by JTC personnel, Article 62 of the contract states: "This contract and its amendments will be written both in Chinese and in English. Both language versions are equally authentic."

To make this provision practical, CFO arranged for an outside law firm with experts in Chinese and English to "conform" the language used. One expert studied the English version of the contract and translated it into Chinese. A second expert studied this Chinese version and translated it back into English. Then the second translation was compared with the original. Where significant differences were found in the two English drafts, and where JTC personnel felt that the Chinese translation did not match their understanding of the intent of a passage, a conference was held to find language that would meet these two tests.

This conforming process proved to be tedious and time-consuming. In fact, the process was not fully completed when the private dinner to mark the signing of the contract was scheduled. However, this was the final step in assuring that a carefully crafted contract was consistently understood by both parties.

Stultz, consistent with his long insistence that known ambiguities should not be disregarded, was unwilling to sign a not quite finished contract. Only after all-night negotiations and an explicit procedure set for settling the few remaining points was the joint venture contract (and associated documents) signed by officials of JTC and CFO. The date was November 21, 1986, two years and five months after CNTC and Celanese had tentatively agreed on the key elements in a cooperative effort that finally emerged as the Nantong Cellulose Fibers Company.

Push for Completion

The end of the approval process did not fall into place automatically. When MOFERT received a completed draft of the contract the people reviewing it raised a long list of questions. These questions implied that the entire concept of the joint venture had to be justified over again. Fortunately most of the points raised had already been considered by the State Planning Commission in its approval of the joint feasibility study. Sponsors of NCFC were able to convince MOFERT that such points did not need to be approved again. Only three questions remained, and the JTC/CFO representatives quickly agreed on relatively simple ways to resolve these. The joint venture contract was approved by MOFERT in a near-record time of six weeks!

This prompt action by MOFERT reflected a lot of careful work prior to submissions of the completed contract for approval. 1) The joint feasibility study was unusually complete and realistic; it settled many issues that otherwise would have been debated by the State Planning Commission. 2) The Chinese lawyer had discussed various ambiguities in Chinese law with people in MOFERT (and other agencies concerned) during the writing of the contract; potential stumbling blocks were identified and removed in this informal process. 3) Celanese lawyers were experts on international practices and suggested concepts and wording that had been tested many times in practice. So the draft submitted to MOFERT was already a polished one.

Conclusions Regarding the Approval Process

The elapsed times between the submission and approval of the NCFC joint feasibility study and the NCFC joint venture contract were fairly short. Even more striking were the limited number of changes required by the approving agencies. To a remarkable extent the standards applied by the approving agencies were anticipated and met in some way prior to the submission of formal proposals.

Several steps taken by the JTC and CFO negotiators contributed to this impressive record.

a. Creative ways were developed for meeting the objectives expressed in the standardized Chinese laws and regulations for foreign joint ventures. For example, output guarantees were made realistic by establishing standards for Chinese inputs as well as final outputs. Foreign exchange was to be generated by import substitution instead of new exports. Competition was introduced early in the planning process rather than expecting each bidder to go through the time-consuming and expensive process that CFO and JTC followed in developing their proposal. Repayment of registered capital at the end of the contract period was made more acceptable by establishing a plan for accumulating the necessary foreign exchange during the period of the contract. And so on.

In general the objectives sought by the drafters of the Chinese laws were met, but not necessarily in the ways originally conceived.

b. Ambiguities in the new Chinese laws and regulations were discussed with the regulators while the joint venture contract was still being drafted. Then acceptable provisions could be written into the draft before it was submitted.

Also gaps in the regulation were covered by customary international practice—which was recognized by the reviewing bodies.

c. Conforming the contract language in the Chinese and the English versions contributed to a mutual understanding of just what was meant. This helped to assure that the two founding parties maintained a united front in seeking approvals.

Although time was consumed in such careful work during the drafting of the documents that were submitted for approval, the prompt approvals resulted in a net gain in time consumed. And by taking the initiative JTC and CFO had more flexibility in how acceptable drafts were achieved.

Guidelines for the future. This experience in obtaining approval of the feasibility study and the joint venture contract for NCFC suggests the following guidelines for other future joint ventures.

1. Take time to think through a practical, realistic joint venture plan which a) serves the interests of both of the founding partners, and b) at the same time supports PRC objectives. Writing documents for

central approval before the basic plan is clear invites questions and delays in the approval process.

2. Approach objectives stated or implied in existing laws and regulations creatively. There probably are several different ways the objectives can be met, and a particular joint venture should select ways that suit its particular situation.

3. Use informal advance discussions with people in the approving agencies when their standards are vague and when unique actions are being considered. Such "testing of the water" may indicate what proposals are likely to be acceptable, and novel proposals will not come to the reviewers as a surprise.

Chapter 13

Conclusion to Part II: From Concept to Contract

A technology/market exchange is the core concept of the agreement struck by CNTC and Celanese in the autumn of 1984. As explained in Part I, Celanese was to provide production technology to a joint venture, and in return CNTC was to make Celanese a preferred supplier of tow for the Chnese market. Within a few months the key features of a new enterprise were agreed upon.

Turning that concept into a practical joint venture contract, however, required a lot of elaboration and refinement. Planning on many dimensions was necessary—as has been explained in the preceding six chapters. Several parts of the joint venture contract that emerged from this planning are quite distinctive, and they should be reemphasized in this brief summary.

Distinctive Features of the NCFC Joint Venture Contract

1. The contract is much *more specific* than many previous Chinese/foreign agreements. Few potentially troublesome issues were left for

"later discussion." Instead, discussions between the two contracting parties continued until a practical and acceptable plan was developed. As a result, the NCFC contract is a comprehensive plan of action, which is clearly stated and mutually acceptable. Because of the time and care devoted to their formulation, the prospects are high for these plans being carried out as intended.

2. The joint venture is designed to perform a *restricted set of activities* for a limited period of time. It is to run a "focused factory," concentrating on the production of cellulose acetate cigarette tow for use within China's domestic market. Since research and development work will be done by Celanese and marketing by CNTC, this particular venture can seek excellence in a well defined niche.

In the future the founding parties may undertake other joint ventures, or agree to extend the life of NCFC. But for the present, NCFC is a self-sufficient, self-liquidating venture. Instead of giving NCFC a wide scope, only part of which can be started soon, the approach is to move forward one step at a time.

This narrower focus makes possible the specific planning noted in point (1) above. It also increases the chances of keeping the venture on track—a difficult task in China's highly dynamic economy.

3. The NCFC contract includes *innovative ways of meeting the objectives* of several recent Chinese laws and regulations for joint ventures without overburdening the company with impractical requirements. Such innovative provisions include the following:

   a. Quality and output guarantees of foreign technology are extended to include comparable requirements for local inputs of heat, power, materials, and other aspects of the setting in which the technology will be used. These extensions protect the foreign supplier of technology (CFO) and, more important, they improve the likelihood that the technology will meet expectations.
   b. The typical requirement for a foreign joint venture to export a sufficient portion of its output to generate foreign exchange needed is replaced by "import substitution" as a source of foreign exchange.
   c. The provision that CFO is to receive compensation at the termination of the joint venture contract after 15 years is coupled with a foreign exchange funding arrangement to assure that hard currency will be available to make the repayment.

d. Since CFO's investment could be considered a long-term loan as opposed to a share in the equity of NCFC, tying membership on the board of directors to investment did not make sense. Instead, an equal number of directors named by CFO and JTC (and unanimous decisions on key actions) was inserted as a way of protecting the interests of both parties.

These features—extending the contract to specific plans, narrowing the scope to a focused factory, being creative in the way PRC objectives are met—illustrate the effort made by JTC and CFO to write a contract that a) is a workable plan, and b) also meets at least the primary objectives of major cooperating organizations.

The NCFC contract is an example of advance planning. Its authors sought to recognize and deal with problems prior to the time when they surface in actual operations. In this respect, the NCFC contract goes a step beyond the usual contract in many foreign joint venture agreements. The contracting parties are ready to act.

Building Consensus While Negotiating

Negotiating an action-oriented joint venture contract, as just suggested, poses some problems. There is an inherent tension between a) seeking ways to increase the total output of cooperative efforts, and b) each party trying to negotiate an attractive deal for itself. The *process of negotiating* affects the balance.

1. *Cultural differences in approach.* Typically, the Chinese place a high value on harmony and avoiding sharp confrontations. If necessary, they tend to postpone win/lose choices or to use vague language where differences in opinions persist. In contrast, Americans usually prefer to bring issues out in the open, and to frankly discuss differences in values or opinions in an effort to find mutually acceptable solutions. Americans do not consider such confrontations to be unfriendly or disrespectful.

In the NCFC negotiations, Stultz and other Americans followed their cultural pattern and sought to have potential problems recognized, discussed, and a resolution written into the joint venture contract. This process led to the unusual specificity in the contract noted in (1) above. However, reaching these written conclusions did take time, and on the part of the Chinese also a tolerance with American abruptness.

2. *Finding mutually acceptable solutions.* Since both Chinese and American personnel involved in the operation of NCFC would be expected to carry out these negotiated solutions, a full understanding and genuine acceptance or commitment became very desirable. To achieve this mutual acceptance an exploration of the objectives, values, costs and other concerns of each side was often necessary. And because of the diversity of cultural background and personal experience, time for an open discussion again became necessary.

The main negotiators for JTC and CFO soon developed this mutual understanding and respect. More difficulty arose with their advisors. Especially on the Chinese side, the technical advisors tended to think only in terms of their specialty and of strict adherence to their interpretation of regulations. The technicians had little incentive to take a broader, empathetic viewpoint.

Fortunately for the workability of the new venture, the main negotiators were executives with general management experience; they had the time and patience to sit through a long series of meetings; and they were skilled in developing a consensus on key issues. So NCFC starts out with joint enthusiasm; it is more than an arranged marriage.

3. *Bargaining and competition.* A deterrent to building close cooperation, suggested in the preceding paragraphs, is bargaining for a better deal for oneself. Partly as a result of a past history of foreign exploitation of China, PRC laws stress safeguards against foreign companies reaping undue advantages in their transactions with China. Limits on the duration and the percentage of foreign participation in joint ventures such as those in the NCFC agreement—reflect this caution.

Another way the PRC buttresses its bargaining strength is to insist that competitive bids be obtained on major agreements. Then one bidder can be played against another to secure for China a better price, investment, or other benefit. Rarely is such bidding open. Rather, both the Chinese and the foreign bidders make guesses about how hard to push the other party on each dimension of a transaction.

An obvious disadvantage of this sort of bargaining is that a frank and honest exploration for mutually acceptable terms of agreement is discouraged. Developing a specific, workable program for a pioneering joint venture—like the one written into the contract for NCFC—is extremely difficult when both parties are thinking primarily about how to secure a bargaining advantage.

In the CNTC/Celanese negotiations for tow production in China, this dilemma regarding the use of bargaining was met in two stages. First, world competition was invited on which company would engage in the detailed planning of a joint venture contract for the Nantong site. And to some extent the competition was kept open by asking different companies to develop plans for plants at the three selected sites—Nantong, Jilin, and Xian.

Second, after Celanese was identified as the company most likely to be an eager joint venture partner at Nantong, an arrangement for cooperative negotiations were pushed down a level to JTC and CFO where both local and corporate factors could be weighed. Also, an optimum cooperative plan of action could be developed because this lengthy negotiation was exclusive; the parties assumed that they were designing a close operating relationship extending over a period of years.

So, both competitive bargaining and joint planning were used. But during the period covered by this study competitive bargaining was eventually set aside. The primary effort has focused on building a strong consensus around a jointly designed action plan.

4. *Getting central organizations to join in the consensus.* China's centralized economic planning coupled with scarce resources inevitably make approval of a joint venture like NCFC a serious matter. The State Planning Commission had to approve the joint feasibility study and MOFERT had to approve the joint venture contract.

Basically the JTC and CFO negotiators sought to cross these hurdles in advance—by taking pains to prepare documents that fit the standards which the reviewing agencies would apply. The complications were that on some matters no general standards existed, and on other matters—such as import substitution of foreign exchange or competitive bids—the NCFC plan met the spirit but not the letter of existing regulations.

So, while the joint feasibility study and the joint venture contract were still being drafted, representatives of the drafting team informally discussed unusual provisions with people within the reviewing agencies. As a result, the finished documents contained few surprises for the central reviewing organizations; most potential objections had already been resolved. Both documents were approved with only minor adjustments.

Note that this procedure did not reduce the combined influence of the reviewing agencies. It just meant that the influence was exerted while the plans were easily adapted. Major benefits from the preliminary discussions, in addition to faster processing, included the building of a widespread consensus around the final plan.

*   *   *

The NCFC joint venture contract was slow in the making—over two years of persistent negotiating. However, it is a focused, practical plan strongly endorsed by the people primarily responsible for its execution.

Part III

From Plans to Delivering Products

When Nantong Cellulose Fibers Company (NCFC) came into existence in March 1987, its most valuable assets were 1) a strong commitment by its founders to make this new joint venture an outstanding technological and economic success, and 2) a specific plan for doing so. Active negotiations extending back to July 1984 had produced a comprehensive agreement on technology transfer, financing, organization, management training, plant design, and a variety of other features of the new company. The time for action had finally arrived.

Several optimistic Chinese talked of production in 1988. Celanese officials were more realistic with a target date early in 1989. In fact, full capacity operations were achieved in October 1989—an impressive accomplishment in view of the difficulties facing Chinese/U.S. cooperative ventures during that period.

The advance planning, written into the joint venture contract, served as a blueprint for the new company during its start-up. Most of the physical design and business structure was already settled, and surprisingly few changes were found to be necessary. The earlier effort devoted to planning paid off.

Nevertheless, a variety of problems arose in the process of execution. Differences between Chinese and U.S. managerial practices and expectations underlay most of these problems. Obligations of construction contractors, the nature of the authority of managers, securing coordination of interrrelated work, the significance attached to finishing work on time, how to deal with cost overruns, the setting of equitable prices—all called for managerial action.

Since guidelines that will be useful in future Chinese/foreign joint ventures—or to similar ventures in other developing countries—is a primary aim of the present study, these cultural hurdles involved in the problem areas just noted should be described in this Part III. Joint action was especially important for activities within the battery limits, so many of our examples will be drawn from that arena.

These construction and start-up problems will be reviewed in the following chapters:

Chapter 14   Constructing a World-Class Plant

Chapter 15   Adjustments in Human and Financial Inputs

A concluding Chapter 16 will then summarize the bases for durable collaboration that gives strength to the Nantong Cellulose Fibers Company.

Chapter 14

Constructing a World-Class Plant

Outstanding success tends to cover up the struggles and the assistance that made the success possible. For instance, the impressive sight of the Nantong plant producing a continuous stream of top-quality tow day after day tends to obscure the actions that helped and hindered getting the plant up and running. Yet for managerial learning key events in the process of building are important.

This chapter focuses on actual construction of the plant. First we note several distinctive contributions to NCFC's successful building program. Making the first tow plant in China a world-class producer within a few weeks of start-up had to have a lot of positive supports. Next we briefly describe several difficulties that occurred along the way and how they were resolved.

Strengths Aiding Erection of the Plant

Several factors that were developed during the prolonged joint venture negotiations paid off during the construction process.

1. The comprehensive written specifications for the buildings, equipment, and support services were based on Celanese's advanced and proven technology. These plans, especially for the processing layout and equipment within the battery limits, were quite detailed to take advantage of Celanese's *long experience* in several different U.S. plants. Similarly, the plans for the large boilers to generate steam and, ultimately, electricity and for water processing reflected successful installations of such equipment elsewhere in China. In other words, the physical features of the desired plant were both wise and clearly stated in considerable detail.

2. The individuals selected for senior management positions in NCFC were very *competent people* with experience that qualified them for their respective assigned duties. Stated another way, the new company was not overloaded with inappropriate executives—i.e., people whose skills and experience did not fit NCFC's needs.

3. *Separate responsibility* within NCFC for getting the plant up and running was wise. An "office for preparation and construction," separated from continuing operations, permitted concentrated attention by a temporary group of construction engineers and project engineers which could be disbanded or reassigned when this major project was completed. At no time was there any doubt about the dominant priority of this office—getting the plant running as specified, on time, within cost limits. Meeting these targets (as revised) would have been much more difficult without this focused attention.

4. Assistance of both local and national government organizations had been prearranged. Necessary allocations of materials and equipment were made substantially as needed. At the local level, the City of Nantong a) allocated land for the plant site and approved the plan for removing residents from the land to newly built housing; b) assigned workers with appropriate education to NCFC; and c) issued or secured necessary permits, etc. Basically *"bureaucracy" did not hinder construction.*

5. CFO supplied expert technical assistance to contractors and JTC during construction. Celanese is a large corporation with a variety of technical skills existing in its many staff units. CFO arranged to have as many as twenty of these experts on the Nantong site at one time. They provided advice and supervision as needed on a variety of

problems. In addition, Foxboro/Shanghai—a U.S. and Chinese joint venture that supplied much of the instrumentation for the Nantong plant—sent several of its engineers to assist in the start-up. Thus, the project had an unusually flexible flow of *relevant technical assistance*.

6. The Chinese engineers who were trained for six months by Celanese in the United States returned to Nantong when construction work was lagging. By then these men and women were familiar with tow technology and Celanese practices, and most of them could discuss these things in English. They provided a unique resource for communication between Celanese experts and Chinese contractors, and for close observation of what was actually happening at many places in the total construction process. While not so planned, the trainees served as a vital *cultural bridge* at a crucial period in the construction process.

7. Constructive *cooperation of NCFC's founders*—CNTC and Celanese—also was a significant help during construction. Although more intangible, their continuing strong support maintained the "full speed ahead" climate. No bickering, or doubt, or threat of withdrawal undercut the morale of people confronting daily problems. And when additional capital became essential to complete the project these organizations worked out a simple arrangement that provided the increased investment.

It is likely that if any one of these supporting factors had been absent, the start-up of NCFC's tow plant would have been seriously delayed.

Experience with Contractors

Even with the favorable help just listed, the "preparation and construction office" faced several difficult hurdles. The most upsetting of these was the way the outside construction contractors performed their work.

As anticipated in the joint venture agreement, JTC signed contracts with two large outside construction firms to do most of the actual work of building the plant. One firm did the "civil" work—creating drainage, laying roads, erecting buildings and other structures, installing basic electrical lines, and the like. The nature of this work was similar to civil construction of most other factories.

The second firm, a ''mechanical'' construction contractor, did the installing of equipment, making the numerous piping connections, adding the control instruments, and otherwise preparing the machinery to operate. While some of this work was similar to the construction of other chemical processing plants, its specific design was unique to tow production.

Both contractors took the view that, having been awarded the contract, it was their right to decide how and when the work was to be done. After all, they were the experts in construction and had learned from other jobs how to proceed. Except for coordination, to be discussed later, this approach worked satisfactorily for the civil contractor. For the mechanical contractor, however, this approach did cause problems.

Two incidents illustrate the kind of difficulties that often arose with the mechanical contractor and its subcontractors. One example deals with placing thermal insulation around a pressure tank. The contractors' men started to put the insulation on before testing the tank and connections for leaks. U.S. and Celanese practice is to test for leaks first, then insulate, especially because of the high pressures this part of the system has to hold. The contractors' men resented the suggestion of a Celanese engineer that the test come first and refused to comply. Only after the Celanese engineer said he would not accept that part of the plant, and after several long discussions were held (via an interpreter), was agreement reached to test the equipment for pinhole leaks in its partially insulated state. The covered-up parts never did get tested for small leaks.

A second incident dealt with installing collars on the central shafts in very large mixing tanks. (The collars hold long blades that do the mixing.) To get a tight fit, such collars are carefully machined to be a bit smaller than the diameter of the shafts. Then just before being slipped onto the shaft the collars are heated and expanded in a hot oil bath; while still hot they slip on easily, and when they cool and contract they bind very tightly around the shaft.

In this case, a Celanese engineer happened to pass by while the contractors' men were trying to drive a cold collar onto a shaft with a sledgehammer. Persistent effort had moved the collar about a sixteenth of an inch. The Celanese engineer protested because he knew the shaft would soon be ruined, and a replacement from outside of China would probably take a month even when shipped airfreight. The men's reply, translated, was: "We often have misfits and know what to do with them." When reasoning did not help, the engineer demanded the use of a hot oil bath. The men just walked away for a long lunch, and the engineer stormed back to his room saying that he would write a letter to JTC to say that CFO could no longer be held to their guarantee of performance. By then, many people in the plant knew of the confrontation.

The Celanese engineer soon realized that protest letters would not get the mixing tanks assembled. So, he tried humor. He sent a messenger to the men with a letter saying, "If you will try the hot bath method on just one collar and it does not work, then I will make a large thirty-foot banner saying in large letters 'Mickey Thinks He Is An Engineer But He Doesn't Know What He Is Talking About' and hang it on the side of the building where everyone can see it." When the engineer walked through the mixing area the next morning there was some oil on the floor and all the collars were in place. Nothing was said about how this happened.

These two incidents were only symptomatic. The mechanical contractor's men continued to work their way, not always meeting written specifications. Trying to get their work finished up so that commissioning and start-up of the plant would take place created a continuous string of stoppages. Finally, the construction office decided to close out the contract as though the work was completed, and then to hire local craftsmen or small contractors to do the finishing work under the close supervision of Celanese engineers and recently returned management trainees. This arrangement worked well; the trainees knew and could communicate the result that was wanted, and the local craftsmen were surprisingly adept at performing the specified tasks.

A complicating dimension of relations with the mechanical contractor was that JTC, which made the contract on behalf of NCFC, was reluctant to press the contractor for correct and prompt performance. This reluctance probably came from several factors:

1. The contractor was a well known organization and did work throughout the region. It seemed that it would have appeared presumptuous for a provincial tobacco company to challenge the way such a contractor did construction work.

2. The contractor was busy and could obtain plenty of other work.

3. Using power, such as withholding payments until work met CFO specifications, just was not customary behavior.

So the task of seeking better performance fell to CFO personnel who were serving in an advisory role. The Americans were baffled about how to get desired results from the contractor. There seemed to be:

a. an unwillingness to use the concept of hierarchical authority— between both the general contractor and subcontractors and a subcontractor and his teams of workers. The professionals at the bottom of the line could do the work in their own way at their own pace;

b. and face-saving was crucial. There should be no outward appearance that any professional was taking instructions from someone else, or had made a mistake.

In such circumstances the most that the Americans could do was to try to make clear *in advance* the desired end result and perhaps the method of achieving it. Then they had to hope that the contractor and his professionals would adjust their actions the following day or two as though any adjustment had been their own choice. Unfortunately, the Americans had little leverage to help get their ideas accepted, and language barriers interfered with open communications.

In the future, perhaps some of these on-the-spot tensions can be reduced if the U.S. company with the technical expertise makes the contract directly with the main contractors, and includes in such a contract a stipulation that foreign engineers can prescribe methods of construction when necessary to achieve the new technology. Whether a large, financially strong general contractor would accept a contract on such terms was not tested in the project we are reporting on here.

Related to the behavior of the mechancial contractor were problems of coordination.

Coordination Difficulties

Coordination of the Nantong plant construction faced two difficulties that are common in China. One is an unrealistic sense of the passage of time. In a country like China getting work done according to a schedule doesn't seem important to many people (including NCFC's contractors). On the other hand, if prompt completion of a project is considered to be desirable, estimates of when the project will be finished tend to be overly optimistic. Estimates of completion dates for stages of the Nantong construction seemed to be either just a wish or a date that the inquirer would like to hear, rather than a considered judgment based on likely delivery of materials and on processing time for blocks of work.

In this setting, use of sophisticated coordination techniques like PERT or critical path analysis could not be applied to construction of the Nantong plant. CFO engineers used Gantt charts for estimating, but the existence of such charts did little to develop strong commitments by people doing the work.

The dovetailing of related work also met resistance. Each contractor or subcontractor proceeded on his assignment with apparent minimum regard for fitting in with work of other contractors. A subcontractor painting the ceiling of a shop, for instance, moved ahead even though paint would be dripped on expensive new equipment just moved onto the floor. To cite another example, the civil contractor poured second-level concrete floors in one building which later had to be partially removed to move in large equipment.—Of course, the unreliability of scheduled times makes synchronized activities hard to achieve.

This experience indicated that some Chinese construction contractors may not have grasped the concept of coordinated project management of a complex job like building the Nantong plant. The idea of centralized coordination by an overall manager of the sequence and timing, step-by-step, is unknown or at least untried. In contrast, if the contractors and the subcontractors could bring themselves to comply with some outside authority over their work—as suggested in the preceding section—then the well developed Western techniques of project management could significantly improve coordination of effort.

Resource Crisis

For reasons noted above, construction of the Nantong plant had fallen seriously behind schedule by the end of 1988. An early start-up target of spring 1989 was clearly unrealistic, and a June date was more of a hope than a careful forecast.

On top of this delay was the mechanical contractor's inability or unwillingness to complete his work in a form that was ready for plant start-up. A proposed use of local craftsmen under trainees' supervision would involve a lot of expense that was not covered in NCFC's budget.

At this juncture, if either CNTC or Celanese had been bargaining for short-run advantage or lacking in mutual trust, a breakdown in the cooperation on the joint venture might have occurred. Fortunately, the relationship between these two founding parties was strong rather than strained, and they were able to quickly find a way to inject more capital into NCFC—as will be explained in the following chapter.

Overcoming the financial crisis in February 1989 gave the necessary support for using local craftsmen to complete the plant as originally planned. With additional money and cooperative manpower, construction moved ahead with renewed speed.

Impact of Tiananmen Square Protest

The incidents of June 4, 1989 in Tiananmen Square, Beijing, threatened to jolt the NCFC building activity in June. Actually, the immediate effect of these incidents in the city of Nantong was minor. Students marched a couple of times; people were tense; but not much more happened in this provincial location.

For NCFC the chief disturbance came from the United States. Acting in the interest of personal safety, CFO promptly brought home a dozen technical experts who were on short assignments in Nantong. However, other U.S. personnel requested permission to stay, at least on a day-to-day basis. Within a couple of weeks the potential danger to foreign experts in China subsided, and Celanese personnel needed at the construction site returned.

By this time most of the actual construction was finished and the process of "commissioning" (final inspecting, testing, adjusting) each part of the plant was underway. All of the Chinese employees who were trained in the United States were back and at work. Morale picked up as the many sections of the total complex began fitting into a working mode. An initial start-up date of September 4th (predicted by a realistic American manager back in March) again seemed possible—and in fact it was achieved.

Snags During Plant Start-Up

Moving from the first through-put to full-scale operations of an integrated plant rarely is smooth. Even with all the planning and testing, the Nantong plant had its snags. On the morning that the first start-up was attempted there was a power failure, shutting down the complete plant. Three days later after the automatic switching apparatus was presumably fixed a second power failure shut the plant again. Fortunately, the second rescue was more successful. There have been few power difficulties after these two early shut-downs.

Another traumatic event bringing the entire plant to a halt was trouble with the baling press. All of NCFC's output must pass through this relatively simple machine. At the end of the first week a bent ram on this baling press had the entire flow stopped—and securing a replacement of the ram from Germany would take twenty weeks.

Instead of waiting for a replacement, a decision was made to try cutting off the end of the ram and welding on a new piece of steel ten inches round and twelve inches long. A large steel bar seventeen inches round and six feet long was located at a shipyard; from this bar the new end was precisely cut and turned down to size in an around-the-clock effort. In four days the baling press was back in operation. Aside from some engineering, the local Chinese did every bit of that ingenious and exacting repair.

In spite of the stumbling blocks such as the two just mentioned, output of the plant improved week by week. By the end of November international quality tow was being produced at a faster rate than the guaranteed capacity of 10,000 tons per year.

Suggested Guidelines for Future Joint Ventures

The preceding review of the construction and start-up of NCFC's tow plant in Nantong indicates that several managerial practices can be very helpful in getting a Chinese plant built and running. At least in this one case the following actions were, or would have been, important contributors to constructing a factory to serve stated goals.

1. Do prepare comprehensive written plans for the buildings, equipment, and auxiliary services—using a tested technology as the base. A foreign location with a foreign partner is a poor setting for designing by trial-and-error.

2. Do establish cooperative relationship with both local and national government organizations whose assistance or approval you may need.

Domestic folkways or regulations may not easily fit the dynamic needs of the joint contract.

3. Do arrange for a diversified array of experienced technical experts from abroad to work at the new site when needed. U.S. technology in one area may unexpectedly call for adjustments in Chinese practice in a related area.

4. Do establish on the site a separate organization unit to supervise and coordinate the whole construction project. Include in this unit both foreigners and nationals—probably from the companies funding the joint venture.

5. Do train in the home-base of the foreign partner a whole core of young Chinese managers and engineers who will become key personnel in the new joint venture. The aim is a) to make these people bilingual in dealing with the induatry and technology of the joint venture; b) to let them see and understand processes used by the foreign partner; and c) to acquaint them with the foreign partner's management practices. Get them back to China while construction of the plant is still in progress.

6. Do reach an agreement with contractors, before they are hired, about a) the role of foreign advisors, b) the criteria for accepting the work of each contractor, and c) withholding payment to each contractor of money needed to cover the costs of correcting and/or completing work as specified.

7. Do try to get understanding and acceptance by each contractor of the scheduling techniques to be used in planning and coordinating the construction activities. (But don't place full reliance on the time commitments implied in these schedules.)

8. Do have an agreement among partners of the joint venture about how overruns of construction budgets, if any, will be confronted. (See Chapter 15 for expansion of this idea.)

9. Do cultivate continuing cooperative relationships among partners of the joint venture which will aid in devising ways to overcome

problems which are not addressed in the joint venture contract and which, inevitably, arise. Even the most carefully written contract will not cover every potential problem that may arise during the project construction.

Chapter 15

Adjustments in Human and Financial Inputs

Overall, the construction of the Nantong plant was completed quite close to the way it was planned. Nevertheless, several unplanned adjustments in size and use of human resources and capital contributions were necessary to finish the project. And NCFC's ability to call on its Chinese/American joint venture sponsors significantly affected the adjustments which emerged.

Crucial Role of Trainees

In any foreign venture reliance on expatriates has limitations. Typical drawbacks are that a foreigner does not fully understand the local language and culture; also a manager or technical expert who expects to return to his home-base is expensive to maintain in a foreign post.

In recognition of these difficulties the NCFC plans provided for training a group of able young Chinese in U.S. plants. In addition to the group which spent at least six months in Celanese U.S. plants, a second group was sent to the United States for six weeks. These people are now familiar with Celanese technology in action; U.S. production processes have become real and doable. As a result of this intensive exposure, the trainees should solve most production problems promptly—and they can train their co-workers to do likewise. Reliance on expatriates can be sharply reduced. Also, because many of these competent individuals combine language skills and technical understanding they can fill "boundary spanning" roles between Chinese and U.S. contributions.

The joint venture plan anticipated that these trainees would serve in key positions for the operation of the new plant. And there is no reason to doubt that they will do so.

Actually they made a crucial contribution before the plant was ready to run. Many of them provided a vital link in the final construction and start-up of the plant. In the gap between the work of the mechanical contractor and a smooth-running plant envisaged by Celanese engineers the trainees provided a crucial bridge. Although not trained for construction work, they were able to understand the technical instructions from Celanese (and Foxboro) experts and translate these instructions into Chinese terms which the local craftsmen could follow. In addition to engineering knowledge and bilingual skills these trainees have an informal sense of Chinese values and attitudes which influence Chinese workers' responses to U.S. management concepts. Without such bridging the start-up of the plant would have been seriously delayed.

The lesson is that, at least in this case, well prepared specifications plus an American engineer to explain them were not adequate to finish up a state-of-the-art plant. Possibly a better understanding with the mechanical contractor would have reduced the gap. However, it is clear that successful transfer of a sophisticated, unfamiliar technology calls for boundary spanning people who can both a) grasp the details of what makes the technology work in the foreign setting and also b) communicate these technical details to Chinese professionals in a manner that they will accept.

The use of trainees for assistance on construction and start-up did involve a cost—cost in the sense that the individuals were not available for training operating personnel as had been planned. Because the plant start-up was delayed this cost was not great. In other circumstances, however—such as the construction of an expansion of the Nantong plant—the withdrawal of trainees from operating jobs to help with the new construction could stretch the trained people too thin to perform both jobs well. U.S./Chinese boundary spanning does take patience and effort.

Reconciling Workers' and U.S. Managers' Expectations

NCFC has a competent group of workers. They have come into an entirely new enterprise, learned how to do new jobs, and share in the experience of bringing output up to planned capacity. The selection and training of these workers is clearly a significant achievement.

This success does not mean that work patterns have fully settled down. Plant and office operations are still maturing. The U.S. managers are still learning what is reasonable to expect of the Chinese workers, and vice versa. This need for reconciling of expectations is illustrated in two practices—the pace of work and standards of housekeeping.

Pace of work. The basic joint venture contract stipulated that the total number of NCFC's employees was to be 343. By the time of its plant start-up the NCFC Board of Directors had raised its maximum to 500, and actual employment was 470. The increase was due partly to the way work outside of the battery limits was structured, partly to the extra effort required to perform a new job compared to an established one and partly to difference in opinions about the concentrated effort that should be expected of a worker. How to deal with this increase in the number of employees above international norms has not yet been resolved.

Another indication of different expectations about work pace is a prevailing opinion that workers and supervisors within the battery limits (under a U.S. deputy general manager) carry heavier loads than do workers and supervisors outside the battery limits (under a Chinese deputy general manager). Jobs within the battery limits of this automated plant are structured in a way that calls for close attention throughout the work shift. The pace of work within the battery, especially during the start-up period, is brisk but there are no pay differentials in recognition of this brisk pace. Perhaps a job within the battery carries more prestige, but it is not clear whether this compensates for more rigorous output norms.

NCFC has recently installed a system of individual employment contracts with each employee. So flexibility does exist to give recognition to differences in the demands of various jobs. For this to be effective, however, expectations throughout the company regarding the pace of work need to be clarified.

We should add that the Nantong plant is automated to the extent that labor expenses are a relatively low percentage of total costs. So the issue of work pace is more one of morale than economics. Companies in other industries may not have this much flexibility in tolerable labor expense.

Housekeeping. A second dimension still to be reconciled between the Chinese and American practice is the simple issue of housekeeping. The Celanese managers are accustomed to keeping their plants neat and clean—for reasons of product quality, employee safety, and equipment maintenance. In contrast, at least during construction, Chinese workers were content to have the plant in what the Americans considered a mess. For instance, trash left around the workplace piled up to the extent that a fire of burning trash threatened some of the work; laborers living in the on-site dormitory left garbage in the hallways; wood scraps created safety hazards.

During regular operations these extremes can be avoided. But as one foreign advisor said, "Within a few years this casual attitude about housekeeping can drift into serious maintenance problems. You can't keep a sophisticated plant in top operating condition without treating it with great respect—even loving care."

A complication in attempting to change housekeeping practice is its pedestrian nature. Workers are likely to feel that certainly this commonplace matter should be left to their discretion. And as already noted, Chinese workers can be quite reluctant about changes in behavior which they feel belongs within an individual's personal domain.

In calling attention to the unresolved work pace and housekeeping issues we are also suggesting that intangible aspects of a joint venture may take time to work out. NCFC is too young to have developed workable resolutions to all such personal values and attitude problems. The company's progress to date with human resources is very impressive indeed; however—as should be expected—the total task is not yet complete.

Financing Overruns of Construction Budget

By the end of 1988 it became clear that the total capital investment in NCFC would be inadequate to complete the Nantong plant. When the mechanical contractor was paid off and dismissed in early 1989 the budgeted construction funds were exhausted, yet the plant was far from ready to operate.

Time might have been spent detailing the causes of this overrun of the budget. But such an investigation was not pursued because an historical analysis would not generate the much needed cash to complete the project.

Instead, a new program for finishing the work with local contractors and professionals was prepared—as noted in the preceding chapter—and the cost of this final stage was estimated. This program showed that an additional cash input of about five percent of the total original investment was needed.

In some joint ventures, cost overruns have led to revisions of their basic contract. But contract revisions take time, and each month of delay reduces sales revenues.

To avoid such a delay, the founding parties agreed simply to make cash contributions to NCFC without changing the joint venture contract in any way. The amount of contribution by CFO and by JTC was to maintain the existing investment ratio of 30.68% and 69.32%, respectively. Each party would treat its contribution as an out-of-pocket expense and not have any direct claim for reimbursement.

This quite simple arrangement made in February 1989 had several advantages. It provided a flow of cash immediately. It avoided spending managerial effort on amending the joint venture contract. It reinforced the feeling that CFO and JTC were partners in a major undertaking and shared in an obligation to provide help when needed. And it boosted the morale of managers and engineers who were struggling to finally complete the plant and get it running.

Treating the cash inputs as contributions had an indirect benefit. Instead of standing idle, the plant started producing tow perhaps half a year sooner; and the profits during this period will increase the net earnings that will be distributed to the two investors. From a strictly financial viewpoint, those additional net earnings probably will be a quite respectable return on the additional cash investment, even though the particular amounts do not show up on the accounting reports.

It is true that fifteen years hence CFO will suffer some loss relative to JTC. At the liquidation of the joint venture, CFO receives certain specified compensation and the remaining assets go to JTC. So by treating CFO's extra cash input as a contribution—not an addition to registered capital—there is no obligation to return that sum to CFO at the time of liquidation. CFO chose not to quibble about this amount at the time of the cash crisis. Instead, CFO pushed for prompt action that would strengthen the NCFC venture. In doing so CFO added to its reputation with CNTC as a good partner with which to do business.

Guidelines for Future Managers

The foregoing experiences with mobilizing resources for the construction of a joint venture plant in China suggest several guidelines for future joint venture managers.

1. When building plants having unfamiliar and sophisticated technology, "boundary spanning" personnel are needed—that is, bilingual people who understand management practices in both the sending and receiving countries. Drawings and specifications, even when accompanied by foreign engineers, are not enough. The critical features of the imported technology need to be understood and incorporated into the local cultural setting.

2. Such boundary spanning personnel should be given time to make sure that the new technology is fully understood and accepted. Rarely can a manager just add this indoctrination to an already busy full-time job.

3. The pace and attitude of local workers about their work is at least partly a matter of custom. When a joint venture is first started, managers should decide how much modification of local customs to undertake. The difficult questions are when acceptance of existing practices will interfere with dependable and efficient operation of the new technology. As soon as necessary changes are identified, worker selection and training should deal with these hurdles as well as the transfer of more objective knowledge.

4. Senior managers of a joint venture should review housekeeping practices as a possible area where change is necessary. A lax attitude about one's workplace may carry over to lax practice in maintaining vital equipment.

5. The joint venture contract should create a financial structure that rewards both parties sponsoring the joint venture when the venture is successful. With this as a base, financial emergencies—which are likely to arise—can be handled with a view of what is good for the venture.

This tends to reduce self-centered bargaining when attention should be focused on overcoming the emergency.

6. Also, when faced with a financial emergency—as NCFC was early in 1989—remember that trying to establish blame for current difficulties rarely overcomes the crisis. Instead of an "You did . . ." and "I did . . ." confrontation, an examination of what can and should *we* do now will probably be beneficial for all parties.

Chapter 16

Conclusions: Bases for Durable Collaboration

Suggestions for joint venture managers have been made throughout this report—at the ends of Parts and of chapters. Another way to draw conclusions from the successful experience of the Nantong Cellulose Fibers Company is to note the bases upon which collaboration was built.

Joint ventures always require cooperation on several fronts. These relationships are often new and, especially in foreign joint ventures, they are both sources of strength and potential trouble spots. So in this concluding chapter we summarize highlights in the interrelations between the Chinese and Americans who were active in the creation of NCFC.

Lessons are suggested in the following areas:

- Interactions between the Chinese and American founding partners.
- Interface between the fledgling joint venture and agencies of the Chinese government.

- Getting Chinese professional service organizations to utilize U.S. technological know-how.
- Managing Chinese and American values and customs at the operating level.
- Using "boundary spanners" as bridges between American culture and aims and Chinese culture and aims.

Interactions Between Chinese and American Founding Partners

Each partner in a joint venture has its own aims and agenda. Sooner or later the joint venture will call for some sacrifice in these private programs, and when the founding partners come from such different backgrounds as China and the United States these strains are likely to be difficult to resolve. To offset these strains, several features of the NCFC joint venture strongly promote continuing cooperation by its partners.

1. NCFC blossomed only after a viable basis for cooperation was devised that fit the specific needs of both CNTC and Celanese. Basically CNTC, through its Jiangsu Province operating company, obtained comprehensive technological aid that will enable China to add filters to more of its cigarettes while reducing the drain on its scarce foreign exchange. Celanese got an immediate market for the output of its excess tow production capacity along with a longer-run prospect for recovering its China investment and a moderate profit.

2. The *timing* of benefits and inputs was also right. If Celanese had been asked to provide most of its inputs of technology and equipment early, but was to receive no benefits until net earnings were distributed several years later, probably the agreement would not have been made. Fortunately, the CNTC tow purchases from Celanese as a preferred supplier were "up front." The cash flow was attractive to Celanese but not burdensome to CNTC because CNTC would have imported tow from some source in any event.

3. In designing the new company—NCFC—negotiators for the founding partners continued this pattern of including provisions that were particularly appealing to one side or the other. For instance, JTC agreed that each partner would name half of the board of directors even though invested capital was provided on a 70%/30% ratio. On the

other hand, CFO agreed to JTC designating both the Chairman and Vice Chairman. CFO agreed to train in the United States an additional twelve Chinese managers; JTC agreed that Celanese technology would be used only in the Nantong plant. JTC agreed to a funding plan to assure foreign exchange to pay CFO's termination compensation at the end of fifteen years, and provision was made to update NCFC's technology throughout the contract period. And so forth.

These arrangements usually were not made as direct trades in concessions. Rather, each partner agreed to provisions that were especially important to the other one. In so doing the agreement became increasingly attractive to the partner, and this improved the probability of cooperation during periods of stress. Thus, each partner made a sizable out-of-pocket cash contribution, without prolonged negotiation, to overcome a cash squeeze just before the Nantong plant was completed.

4. Several provisions of the NCFC agreement help to keep the joint venture attractive to both partners.
   a. The agreement lays out plans for the management, facilities, and operatins of NCFC in more detail than do most Chinese/U.S. joint venture agreements. Tough decisions have been confronted and settled wherever possible. As a result, the plans are more realistic and the partners know better what is expected of them.
   b. The agreement concentrates on a single focused-factory. No vague commitments about the future are made. Although both partners do expect the scope of cooperation to expand, the present agreement is not cluttered with unresolved future prospects.
   c. There is an absence of clever devices which might give one partner an unexpected advantage over the other. Instead, the agreement reflects "mutual trust" between the partners.

Of course, the main test of the joint venture agreement will take place over its span of fifteen years. Nevertheless, the formative period from the first serious discussion in July 1984 of a possible joint venture to tested plant operations in January 1990 does indicate that the two main actors have developed a good basis for cooperation during the longer period.

Summarizing: Although the negotiations of the joint venture contract did take about two years to reconcile the quite different views of the Chinese and American founding partners, the document that emerged is upbeat. Instead of emphasizing protection from exploitation, key provisions make NCFC especially attractive to one or both partners. Continuing cooperation is encouraged by enhancing the benefits each partner gets from supporting NCFC.

Obtaining Government Support

A basis for continuing cooperation of the joint venture partners— such as just reported for CNTC and Celanese—is crucial, but it is not enough to assure success. Other interrelations must be established.

In China especially the government and its agencies must endorse and aid the new venture conceived by the partners. NCFC obtained such support in at least five ways.

1. The central purpose of the venture, local production of cigarette tow, is a step in China's long march of economic modernization. The Nantong tow plant fits into the national program for the tobacco industry. So central government backing comes from aiding an already established thrust to improve the quality of cigarettes, reduce the drain on China's foreign exchange, and strengthen the tobacco industry.

Even more specifically, building a tow plant in Nantong was an identified goal before Celanese showed any interest. Celanese entry made this goal attainable. Moreover, the creation of a new, high-status corporation (CNTC) to administer the tobacco monopoly simplified the task of the new joint venture—by establishing a dependable market for both locally produced and imported tow, and by coordinating actions of several central Ministries as well as many local cigarette plants.

Thus, NCFC won government support by fitting into an established government program for the tobacco industry. NCFC did not undertake a more ambitious task of changing that basic program.

2. Nevertheless, to achieve that primary target of a world-class tow plant operating in Nantong several generalized government policies had to be modified. The joint venture agreement devised by CNTC and Celanese did not conform to all the guidelines set forth by various agencies of the Chinese government. Important areas where some adjustments were necessary included the following:
   a. One announced principle is that foreign joint ventures in China should export enough of their products to get foreign exchange needed to pay the foreign partner. The NCFC agreement, how-

ever, relies on "import substitutions" instead of exports to generate foreign exchange. The proposition that a dollar saved (by lowering imports of tow) is as good as a dollar earned (by exports of tow) had to be accepted by government officials.

b. Since the Chinese standard for the discounted rate of return on an investment is well below Celanese's standard, some additional benefit to Celanese is necessary. This takes the form of a CNTC commitment to use Celanese as a preferred supplier of tow (above the output of the Nantong plant). Such a longer-term commitment is uncommon for the Chinese.

c. For major deals the Chinese want proposals from at least three suppliers. Although CNTC did discuss a joint venture for tow with three large companies in addition to Celanese, a *joint* feasibility study was prepared only with Celanese. The Chinese officials had to accept this single study as fair and "competitive."

These deviations from what the Chinese government would like to have as standard practice appear to a foreigner as minor adaptations; yet for a country cautiously experimenting with foreign joint ventures they might have become major obstacles. The State Planning Commission's willingness to make such adaptations indicates the value it attached to moving ahead with construction of a local tow plant and also a high regard for Celanese as a joint venture partner. In this instance, at least, there was flexibility in the Chinese bureaucracy.

3. Government approval of the new joint venture was simplified by closely integrating three key documents: the technology transfer contract, the joint feasibility study, and the joint venture contract. Each of these documents might have gone through a separate, time-consuming review and approval process.

Instead, the negotiators for JTC and CFO included the principal elements of the technology transfer contract as part of the joint feasibility study that was submitted to the State Planning Commission. Also, the joint feasibility study had many sections which were easily written into the draft of the final joint venture contract.

A result of this merging of documents was that the State Planning Commission's approval of the joint feasibility study also constituted approval of the technology transfer plan and of the main provisions in the joint venture contract. And when the joint venture contract was submitted to MOFERT its review could move promptly because only procedural matters remained to be approved.

4. A further aid to smooth relationship with government bodies was informal review of non-standard provisions and wording *prior* to submission of the completed documents. CNTC checked with a representative of the State Planning Commission about adaptations of standardized policies. Also a lawyer with previous experience in MOFERT helped to draft the joint venture contract in language that was understood and acceptable to MOFERT.

These informal reviews identified troublesome passages early when modifications could be made with no loss of face. There were few surprises when the reviewing agencies saw the final documents, and when the agencies' responses went back to the negotiators.

Summarizing, the combined effect of NCFC fitting neatly into government plans for the tobacco industry, a flexibility on the part of government agencies to adapt to particular provisions necessary to make NCFC viable to its founding partners, the integration of key documents requiring government approval, and informal prior reviews of novel provisions in these documents—all contributed to constructive relationships between NCFC and the national Chinese government. Indirectly, the government significantly influenced the provisions of the joint venture agreement, but bureaucracy did not undercut or greatly slow down a viable agreement.

5. The support of local government, as well as national government, is crucial to a successful joint venture. At the local level NCFC's government relations have been good since the start of negotiations.

A key factor in creating this cooperative relationship was holding many of the actual JTC/CFO negotiations in Nantong and Nanjing—the capital of Jiangsu Province. Jiangsu Tobacco Company represented CNTC, and the chief Chinese negotiator maintained close contact with officials in the city of Nantong. Thus, plans for the plant were based on the specific site which the city is providing and on the local labor supply. City officials know what to expect from the presence of the new tow plant and they are preparing for a major addition to the city's economic activity.

Broadly speaking, NCFC's relations with the local government, like its interactions with the national government, have not been tense and dramatic. Rather, the new venture and its founding partners have carefully sought to fit into the host situation as a constructive influence. When modifications of current practices have seemed to be necessary for the creation of a world-class business, these have been requested; but the approach has consistently been one of cooperation and mutual long-run benefit. Thus far this approach, while sometimes tedious, has worked very well.

Relations with Professional Service Organizations

In China, as in the United States, a company building a new plant relies on professional engineering firms and contractor firms to perform most of the design and actual construction work. This was a troublesome relationship for the Nantong project. For work done in China, JTC employed the Chinese firms, and CFO engineers served as advisors to them.

During the preparation of the joint feasibility study (after unsatisfactory starts with two other engineering institutes) an industry engineering institute (IEI) was employed to advise JTC and to prepare designs and specifications for all construction outside the battery limits of the new plant. Two sorts of problems arose in this relationship with IEI.

First, IEI considered its role to be—not an advisor to JTC—instead, an outside agency to certify that the technology to be transferred met all the Chinese government standards for foreign technology transfers. In this role IEI persistently questioned, month after month, the efficiency of Celanese technology (even though Celanese had been selected as a desired partner partly because of its proven technology). The fact that Celanese was to be a partner in the joint venture that would use the technology did not modify IEI's adversarial stance. Only at Celanese's request did JTC finally call a halt to this time-wasting questioning.

The second sort of difficulty arose later when design specifications were being prepared for various parts of the plant. A U.S. firm, under Celanese direction, was doing this work for equipment within the battery limits, while IEI was preparing specificatins for construction and equipment outside the battery limits. In the U.S. two such firms working on interdependent parts of a single project frequently exchange drawings and discuss coordination of related features. In contrast, IEI was unwilling to show any of its drawings to the U.S. engineering firm until all of its assignment was completed. Thus, there could be no coordination while the engineering work was in progress.

Both of these difficulties indicate that IEI perceived its role as a separate organization with its own ideas of what needed to be done. Instead of being a service to JTC, its professional allegiance appeared to lie elsewhere. Celanese engineers found this attitude hard to appreciate.

The construction firm that JTC employed as the senior mechanical contractor in building the Nantong plant also followed an independent course—with more serious results. Around major holidays, construction supervisors and workers were likely to disappear a week early and return a week late. Suggestions by Celanese engineers about how to assemble special equipment were rejected. Sections of work were left untested, and in the view of Celanese engineers unfinished. Occasionally specifications were ignored. More generally, experienced personnel of the mechanical contractor felt that they knew what was wanted and they did it their way. In this sense, they were not cooperative.

Unfortunately, such behavior was unwarranted. The construction fell behind schedule. The contract payments were exhausted, and the contractor was leaving before the equipment was ready to operate. JTC apparently felt that it lacked power to insist that the contractor stay until the plant was running. So the contractor was paid off and an emergency program had to be launched to complete the project.

This crisis was due partly to a misunderstanding about how far the contractor's responsibility extended; also the role of Celanese engineers was not clear. More basic, however, the contractor did not act as a member of a team committed to building a world-class plant. Instead, the contractor's view seemed to be that it had accepted a separate job—on which it would apply its professional experience to the extent that competing pressures could permit; having been selected for the job the contractor felt that other people were not to interfere with how the work was done or when it was done; and after devoting a reasonable amount of effort on the work the contractor felt that it had no further obligation.

To Celanese personnel, who focus more on teamwork to achieve a target result, the contractor's attitude lacked a vital sense of "responsibility." The contractor's attitude was a sharp contrast to the mutual commitment that had developed between JTC and CFO. And it is still not clear what JTC or CFO might have done to get the contractor to join their team.

Dealing with Cultural Differences

Interwoven with relationships between organizations, discussed above, are the widespread cultural attitudes and practices of individuals. Where such personal attitudes and practices of Americans and of Chinese differ, business efficiency may suffer. Examples of potential sources of friction which appeared during the launching of NCFC include the following.

Personal Confrontations

A Chinese Deputy General Manager of NCFC observed, "In China if another person argues with you, you assume that the person dislikes you and will try to block your progress. I had to learn that an American may argue with you about some point but still be your friend."

This Chinese attitude about stating a different opinion makes full and candid analysis of any issue difficult, especially for an American. The American must be very careful how he states a disagreement. A blunt challenge can undermine future cooperation.

A related matter is "loss of face." It is very impolite in China to show publicly that another person was wrong about some facts or made a mistake in judgment. Such an open statement is considered an insult by the erring person and by others who hear it. So the Chinese feel that the error should not be mentioned at all or be covered up in a different approach to the situation under review. For an American who has been taught to seek out and deal with "the facts," saving someone's face—even his own—may interfere with an objective analysis and a wise decision.

One way to avoid loss of face is to not link individuals with determination of facts or with specific decisions. Unfortunately, this tactic muddies "responsibility"—another disagreeable subject to many Chinese.

Deference to Status

During the planning and construction of the Nantong plant several problems called for modifications of policies or regulations issued by national organizations. Yet the Chinese working on the project were quite reluctant to ask the agencies with higher status for relief. Even when the large mechanical contractor failed to do acceptable work, the local Chinese organization that employed the contractor did not press the contractor to finish jobs properly.

In such circumstances the typical American would have at least raised the issue with supervising managers, and if the need was high he probably would appeal to managers on up the line. For Americans to hear "That isn't done in China" left the Americans feeling frustrated.

Partly, such deference in China to high status probably reflects the custom of avoiding confrontations. In addition, there seems to be a Chinese cultural pattern of accepting instructions politely with a minimum of discussion. In contrast, in the United States the popular practice of "consultative supervision" is frequently extended to any source of instructions.

We did observe a safety valve. While the Chinese give deference to persons of higher status, the operating people in the lower levels of the hierarchy do not always follow the instructions. They don't object; they just do things their way, or maybe not at all. (Such practice was clearly noticeable among the construction personnel within the battery limits at Nantong.)

A serious drawback of such deference-but-not-obedience is that a manager cannot rely on work being done as planned. And foreign managers are especially handicapped because their inability to speak Chinese is an additional barrier. The lack of well developed managerial control techniques also confounds the situation.

Fortunately in the Nantong plant construction, the corps of Chinese managers that had received U.S. training returned just when the lack of responsiveness to managerial direction reached a crisis. These men and women did raise questions about what needed to be done until they understood and accepted the instructions. And then they were able to supervise the actual work closely enough to control what happened.

The Time for Decision

In China a different source of slow response to managerial direction is postponing difficult decisions. Many joint ventures run into serious problems because the negotiators of their joint venture contracts often say, "We'll decide that later." As already noted, especially the Chinese wish to avoid confrontations and arguments. So when an issue arises about, for example, the source of foreign exchange or representation on the board of directors, a settlement is postponed. Postponing may avoid an unplesant clash today only to arise later when effort and money have already been expended.

NCFC has faced few problems of this sort. Robert Stultz, the Celanese chief negotiator, insisted that important issues be faced and resolved while the joint agreement was still being formulated. This practice extended the duration of the negotiations, but it also saved time and hard feelings later. Once the comprehensive contract was signed, all parties could focus on getting the new company into operation—without bargaining and discord over issues that had been "swept under the rug" earlier.

A related device used in the NCFC negotiations was preparing memorandums of agreement at the close of each two- or three-day negotiating session. The total negotiations took place over two years—a period long enough for memories to be selective about what had been said months before. Also, Americans tend to think in logical sequences, whereas Chinese—and other Easterners—tend to think holistically (each part is dependent on the other parts) so that no decision is firm until related decisions are made. These two different thought patterns cause difficulty over when an agreement on some point is firm and settled, or when that point is still open for further negotiation.

The use of written memorandums of agreement were very helpful in bringing the complex NCFC discussions to a harmonious close. They made it possible for negotiators to expect that decisions made at an earlier date were still effect.

Work Ethic

Differences exist between the expectations of the typical Chinese and American over what is a "good day's work." Clearly the pace of work within the battery limits of the Nantong plant is faster than the pace outside the battery; an American supervises the former and a Chinese the latter. Also there is a difference in standards for housekeeping, which over the years is likely to influence the maintenance of sophisticated equipment.

Since labor expense is a relatively small part of the total expense of a plant such as the one at Nantong, output per man/day is not really critical. However, variations in workloads within the plant might cause labor unrest if it is viewed as unfair by the workers. So some leveling of workloads probably should be made.

Much more important is the attitude toward working at NCFC which will permeate the entire organization. Perhaps NCFC will be veiwed simply as a place that provides ordinary jobs. Or, NCFC might be considered a national model for modernized plants; working there would be a source of personal pride; keeping the plant in tip-top condition would be an act of respect—almost reverence; the workers would expect to behave as members of an elite corps. This latter attitude—perhaps closer to the Japanese work ethic than the Western work ethic—could emerge by removing the split in viewpoints currently found in the NCFC plant.

Planning Ahead

China has been through so many changes in its business structure during the past fifty years that its business managers have had limited experience in longer-range planning. Estimates for the future of a company tend to be optimistic hopes more than realistic plans. Sometimes the estimates are influenced more by what some goverment official would like to hear rather than by a careful calculation of resources and time needed to achieve a selected goal. The direction may be clear but the predicted timing and size of changes have shaky foundations.

In contrast, U.S. estimates are more dependable, at least for a project like building the Nantong plant. Managers who make these predictions can rely on a bank of experience, and they expect to be held accountable for results being fairly close to estimates.

As a result, the whole attitude about long-range planning in China and the U.S. differs. In the U.S. mangers feel a strong commitment to make the plan happen. Since the plan is considered to be realistic, managers are expected to take whatever initiative is needed to achieve the forecasted result. They are expected to be aggressive, even stepping on a few toes if necessary.

For the Chinese manager, long-range plans usually lack a carefully calculated realistic base, and pushing hard for achievement may involve behavior that is socially unacceptable. So, here again joint venture managers have to develop ways to reconcile approaches coming from quite different cultural backgrounds.

*   *   *

Identifying cultural differences like those noted above does not mean that one is right and the other is wrong. Rather, awareness of such differences regarding personal confrontations, deference to status, the time for decision, work ethic, or planning ahead serves two purposes:

a. Managers in companies with employees from two or more cultures need to understand why their colleagues may act in unfamiliar ways.

b. *If* some cultural pattern is incompatible with the managerial style of a manager, then ways should be sought to either change the managerial style or the cultural pattern—depending on which sort of change will result in the best overall results.

Need for Boundary Spanners

The relationships reviewed in this concluding chapter—between the founding partners, between the embryo company and government bodies, between that company and professional service organizations, and between people from different cultures—all require boundary spanning.

The process of boundary spanning builds a bridge between two different organizations or between two or more people coming from different cultures. Boundary spanners—the persons who perform the bridging activity—need several talents: 1) An empathetic understanding of the customs, values, beliefs, resources, and commitments of people and organizations on each side of the boundary; 2) understanding of the technical issues involved in the relationship; and 3) ability to explain and intrepret both 1) and 2) to people on both sides of the boundary.

Single persons who can be effective boundary spanners in foreign joint venture situations are rare. So often a person with technical knowledge has to be teamed up with one or two people who know local languages and cultures. But it is the intimate combination of the three talents listed in the preceding paragraph that is essential for good boundary spanning.

NCFC owes its existence and operating performance to skillful boundary spanning. Building bridges has been essential at each stage of NCFC's development.

Celanese and CNTC would not have even begun to negotiate their joint venture agreement without the skillful intervention of Steven Perry aided by Katy Coe—both of London Export Company. Because

Perry understood the situation facing each of the partners he was able to devise a workable basis for the joint venture agreement. Then he used his communication skills to help each partner to recognize the potential benefits of intensive negotiations.

The actual negotiation of the comprehensive NCFC joint venture contract proceeded with no major conflict between the partners to a large extent because Katy Coe served as a boundary spanner. She provided Celanese with perceptive insights about Chinese culture, and was a trusted interpreter of issues to both Celanese and CNTC.

During the latter part of the plant construction phase a different sort of boundary spanning became crucial. Technical instructions from English-speaking engineers had to be interpreted and explained to local Chinese construction teams. And, specific difficulties faced by the teams had to be quickly and clearly reported back to the engineers. Here a group of Chinese managers who had just returned from six months training in Celanese plants in the United States stepped into the breach as boundary spanners. They had just learned—in English—the Celanese approach to each step in the chemical process, and they knew Jiangsu-spoken Chinese and culture.

The most extensive boundary spanning during the entire project was performed by Robert Schultz, Celanese chief negotiator. With the help of Coe in communicating with Chinese individuals, Stultz personally spanned all the boundaries. This included not only bridging the U.S. and Chinese points of view. In addition, Stultz spanned the headquarters/field viewpoints within Celanese; and, thanks to an engineering education plus experience as a senior executive in international marketing, he bridged the functional fields of engineering, finance, marketing, and management. Experts were consulted in all these areas but it was Stultz who could understand the language and issues of each area and integrate them into a workable structure.

Of course other boundary spanning occurred—for example between divisions within CNTC, and between CNTC and key sections of the State Planning Commission, and between JTC and MOFERT. The above examples, however, are sufficient to show how vital boundary spanning is to launching an international joint venture. NCFC's success, and its problems, reflect to a significant degree the quality of the boundary spanning in the respective areas.

Index